A Good Read 3

Book 3

Developing Strategies for Effective Reading

Carlos Islam

Carrie Steenburgh

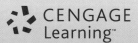

CENGAGE
Learning

Australia • Brazil • Japan • Korea • Mexico • Singapore • Spain • United Kingdom • United States

A Good Read 3
Developing Strategies for Effective Reading
1st Edition
Carlos Islam
Carrie Steenburgh

ELT Publishing Director:
Paul Tan

Senior Product Manager:
Michael Cahill

Editorial Manager:
Edward Yoshioka

Associate Development Editor:
Andrew Jessop

Assistant Editor:
Soh Yuan Ting

Senior Publishing Executive:
Gemaine Goh

Designer:
Redbean De Pte Ltd

Illustrator:
Ng Huk Keng

Cover Images:
Getty Images Sales Singapore
Pte Ltd

ISBN-13: 978-981-4246-97-2
ISBN-10: 981-4246-97-2

Cengage Learning Asia Pte Ltd
5 Shenton Way #01-01
UIC Building
Singapore 068808

Cengage Learning is a leading provider of customized learning solutions with office locations around the globe, including Singapore, the United Kingdom, Australia, Mexico, Brazil, and Japan.

Locate your local office at: **www.cengage.com/global**

Cengage Learning products are represented in Canada by Nelson Education, Ltd.

For product information, visit **www.cengageasia.com**
The publisher would like to thank the following for their permission to reproduce photographs on the following pages:

© 2008 Jupiterimages Corporation: 22; 23; 25; 30; 36; 39; 42; 44; 52; 53; 55; 67; 68; 75; 83; 86; 87; 89; 92; 98; 100; 103; 108; 117.

© 2008 Getty Images Sales Singapore Pte Ltd: cover; 27; 47; 58; 59; 70; 93; 101; 106; 111; 114.

Please note that all people shown are models and are used only for illustrative purposes.

Printed in Singapore
1 2 3 4   12 11 10 09

Dedication and Acknowledgements

We owe a great debt of gratitude to Chris Sol Cruz, Sean Bermingham and Ian Purdon at Cengage Learning. This project owes its life and direction to Chris' initial trust and backing. Sean has steered us through our growing pains while Ian has held our hand nurturing A Good Read with his invaluable insights and suggestions.

We thank all the students at Union County College who piloted much of the material in this series and whose feedback has been crucial.

We would also like to thank our parents for giving us our lives and our characters.

We dedicate this book to our beautiful daughter, Sophia Katherine Islam.

The publisher would also like to thank the following people for their assistance in developing this series:
Chiou-lan Chern, National Taiwan Normal University
Nancy Garcia, Riverbank High School
Brian Heldenbrand, Jeonju University
Kristin Johannsen
Kevin Knight, Kanda Gaigo Career College
Debra J Martinez
Ahmed M. Motala, University of Sharjah
Tufi Neder Neto, Colégio Loyola
Chris Ruddenklau, Kinki University
Scott Smith, Hongik University
Vilma Sousa, Colégio Rio Branco
Naowarat Tongkam, Silpakorn University
Nobuo Tsuda, Konan University
Cally Williams, Newcomers High School
Young Hee Cheri Lee, Reading Town USA English Language Institute
Zainor Izat Zainal, Universiti Putra Malaysia
Vilma Zapata, Miami-Dade County Public Schools

Contents

Welcome to A Good Read!

To the Student:

Reading is a very important part of language learning. Studies show that the more you read, the more you will improve your general English language ability. Through reading, you will build your vocabulary, increase your understanding of grammar, and improve your writing.

In this series, you will find:
- **interesting texts**, on topics such as making money, life-changing moments, and food extremes.
- simple explanations of **reading strategies** (ways you can read a text to help understanding), and activities to help you practice these strategies.
- activities to help you recognize and understand word chunks (words that go together), for example, "black and white," "fast car," "spend time," that will help develop your vocabulary.

By practicing reading strategies and learning **word chunks**, we think you will become a much better reader: You will be able to understand more and enjoy more of what you read.

Good luck,
Carrie and Carlos

To the Teacher:

What do students really need to help them become better readers of English?

A Good Read is designed to help your students become better readers by presenting and practicing reading strategies more explicitly and deliberately than other reading series. These strategies range from core reading techniques—such as skimming and scanning, through "guessing" strategies—such as inferring and predicting, to "personal or reflective" strategies—such as visualizing and summarizing. By learning and practicing these strategies, your students will be able to read more naturally, effectively, and fluently.

In addition, the Word Work activities accompanying each reading have been included to encourage your students to recognize and understand word chunks (groups of words that are frequently found together in texts). Examples of word chunks are "black and white," "leave home," and "first of all." Experts[1] suggest that noticing word chunks improves reading as well as other language skills, as students remember language as whole chunks, not individual words. This saves the reader time and mental energy when reading so that they become more fluent and effective readers.

Carrie and Carlos

---

[1] Lewis, M., 1993, The Lexical Approach, Hove: Language Teaching Publications

Key Features

Start thinking about the unit topic and related language.

Learn how to use each unit's reading strategy.

Think about the reading and related language.

Practice reading strategies covered earlier.

You will read two texts in each unit.

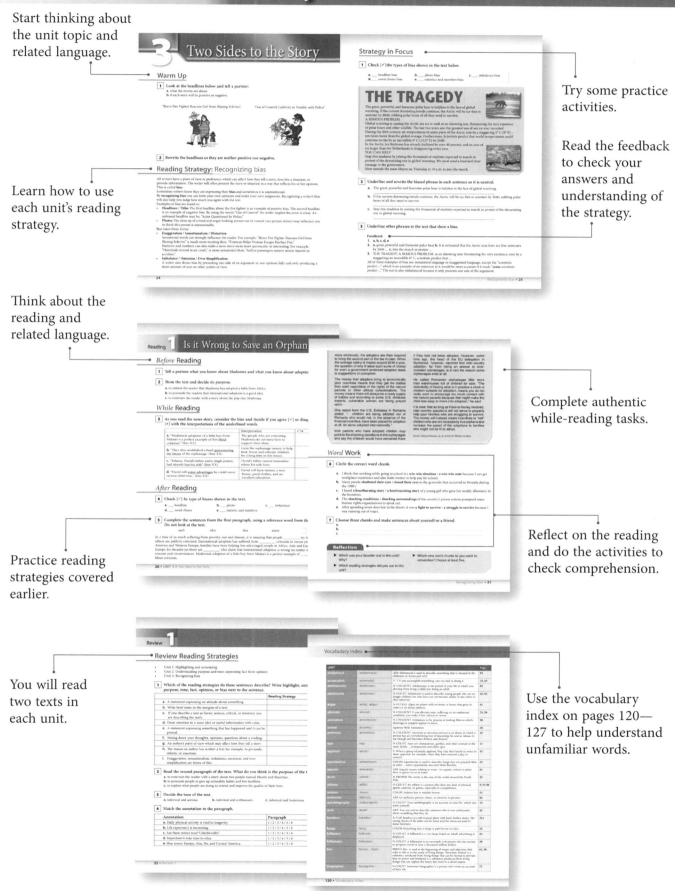

Try some practice activities.

Read the feedback to check your answers and understanding of the strategy.

Complete authentic while-reading tasks.

Reflect on the reading and do the activities to check comprehension.

Use the vocabulary index on pages 120—127 to help understand unfamiliar words.

1 Who's Intelligent?

Warm Up

1 Match the type of intelligence (1-8) to its definition (a.-h.).

1. Kinesthetic - Body Smart
2. Linguistic - Word Smart
3. Logical - Number Smart
4. Interpersonal - People Smart
5. Intrapersonal - Myself Smart
6. Musical - Music Smart
7. Naturalistic - Nature Smart
8. Spatial / Visual – Picture Smart

a. _____ I prefer mathematics to writing essays.

b. _____ I like to see charts and diagrams when I am learning.

c. _____ I like being outdoors when I learn.

d. _____ I would rather work on my own than in a group.

e. _____ I learn more studying and working in groups.

f. _6_ I remember telephone numbers by repeating them to a rhythm.

g. _____ I have a good sense of balance and I move around a lot when I am thinking.

h. _____ I enjoy reading, writing, and talking about things.

2 What are your strongest intelligences? Compare with a partner.

Reading Strategy: Highlighting and annotating

Highlighting the significant parts of a text while reading helps you to:
- distinguish important from unimportant information.
- remember important information.

It is important to only highlight useful information and NOT to highlight too much. Some things that might be useful to highlight are main ideas, definitions, names, dates, events, lists, summaries, and conclusions.

Annotations are brief notes written by the side of a text or in the page margin.

Annotating the text helps you keep your reading active and like highlighting, making annotations helps to distinguish and retrieve important information. Annotations comprise:
- Key words—if a text contains a lot of facts, you can indicate in the margin where these facts appear. For example, next to statistics and facts about the population of Tokyo, you could write "Tokyo facts." Or, you could show where the main idea is by writing "main idea" in the margin.
- Your questions and comments—it is also useful to write your personal responses in the margins. You might write a thought or opinion like "this cannot be true" or "this is the same in my country." The judgments, interpretations, inferences, and associations you make while reading a text are useful annotations to make in the margins.

Tip: It is a good idea to **skim** the text before highlighting or annotating.

Feedback to Warm Up:
1. a. 3;   b. 8;   c. 7;   d. 5;   e. 4;   f. 6;   g. 1;   h. 2.

Strategy in Focus

1 Look at the highlighted (underlined) text and the annotations. Decide why the reader made each highlight and annotation. Choose reasons from the box below.

judgment	association	interpretation	inference	fact
main idea	date	name	definition	

a. _____ b. _____ c. _____ d. _____

e. _____ f. _____ g. _____ h. _____

i. _____

Multiple Intelligence

Throughout our lives, we are faced with many different learning experiences. Some of these experiences have made more of an impact than others. This can be attributed to different intelligences or learning styles. (a) A person's learning style or 'intelligence' is the method through which they gain information most easily. The theory of multiple intelligences was developed in (b) 1983 by (c) Dr. Howard Gardner when he was professor of education at Harvard University, and it suggests that traditional ideas about intelligence, measured by standardized I.Q. tests, are very limited. He proposes eight different intelligences to describe the range of different abilities in children and adults. These intelligences are: (d) linguistic, mathematical or logical, spatial, bodily or kinesthetic, musical, interpersonal, intrapersonal, and naturalistic.

American schools and culture focus attention on linguistic and mathematical intelligence so people who are more articulate or logical are treated differently: they tend to get more respect and are offered better rewards and opportunities. However, (f) Dr. Gardner says that we should place equal attention on people who possess the other intelligences: the artists, musicians, naturalists, designers, dancers, and athletes. Unfortunately, many children don't receive much reinforcement for these abilities in school. Many of these kids, in fact, end up being labeled underachievers because they are taught in a heavily linguistic or logical-mathematical classroom and not in a style appropriate to their type of intelligence.

> **(e.)** This is true for my country too.

> **(g.)** MI would help more students to learn more and get better grades at school.

Education can be much more interesting and help more students learn more effectively if teachers are encouraged to present lessons in a wide variety of ways using music, group work, art activities, role play, multimedia, and field trips among others. The good news is that in America, hundreds of schools are currently using the philosophy of multiple intelligence to redesign the way they educate children. By reaching a range of intelligences, all students will perform better and retain more important information. Understanding a student's learning style can also help later in life and lead them into a more fulfilling career direction.

Many adults find themselves in jobs that do not make the best use of their most highly developed intelligences. For example, the highly bodily-kinesthetic person who is stuck in a linguistic or logical office job would be much happier in a job where they could move around, such as a sports coach, recreational leader, a forest ranger, or physical therapist. The theory of multiple intelligences gives adults a whole new way to look at their lives, examining potentials that they left behind in their childhood (such as a love for art or drama); they may now have the opportunity to develop these through courses, hobbies, or other programs of self-development.

> **(h.)** I completely agree. It would have worked well in my school.

> **(i.)** Someone unhappy in their job.

Feedback

a. definition b. date c. name d. fact e. association

f. main idea g. inference h. judgment i. interpretation

Comparing Chimps to People

Before Reading

1 Tell a partner anything you know about monkeys and intelligence.

2 Take two minutes to skim the text. What is it about? Check [✓] the best answer.

a. _____ Scientists think that in the future, apes may develop to be more intelligent than human beings.

b. _✓_ Scientists are discovering that apes have intelligences and behaviors that are surprising.

While Reading

3 Read the article quickly and without stopping. While reading, decide if your answer to question 2 is correct.

After Reading

4 Highlight the key ideas in the text.

5 Match the annotation to the paragraph and check [✓] the annotation types.

	Annotation	Paragraph	Judgment	Association	Interpretation	Inference
a.	A photographic memory would be useful for studying and work. How would it be useful for monkeys?	2		✓		
b.	Chimps can count to nine and remember the position of numbers but it doesn't seem they can do calculations.	5			✓	
c.	'the chimps left the humans standing' must mean they performed much better than the humans.	7				✓
d.	The experiment in Uganda is more interesting than the one in Japan.	10	✓			
e.	Altruism might be something humans received because chimpanzees are our ancestors.	8		✓		✓

6 Decide if the statements are true (T) or false (F), according to the text.

a. T (F) Chimps can perform calculations faster than people.

b. (T) F The chimps in Dr. Matsuzawa's experiment could count to nine.

c. (T) (F) Felix Warneken thinks that primates (chimps) are not like humans at all and will only help other chimps.

CD 1:
Track 1

Comparing Chimps to People

[1] Few people believe that apes can be smarter than humans. However, scientists are discovering that apes are not only much more intelligent than we had realized, but they also share some surprising behaviors that were previously thought to be unique to humans.

[2] In experiments conducted by Japanese researchers, three chimpanzees beat university students in a memory test. The chimps were able to perform well even when given just a fraction of a second to remember the position of numbers on a screen, suggesting that chimps may have a photographic memory; they remember everything they see.

[3] "There are still many people, including many biologists, who believe that humans are superior to chimpanzees in all cognitive functions [ability to think]," said Tetsuro Matsuzawa, of Kyoto University. "No one can imagine that chimpanzees—young chimpanzees at the age of five—have a better performance in a memory task than humans.

[4] "Here we show for the first time that young chimpanzees have an extraordinary working memory capability for numerical recollection—better than that of human adults tested in the same apparatus, following the same procedure."

[5] Dr. Matsuzawa and his colleagues tested three pairs of chimpanzees, three mothers and their five-year-old offspring. They compared the chimps' performance in a memory task involving numbers with the results of a group of university students doing the same task. The chimpanzees had already been taught to "count" from one to nine. During the experiment, each subject was presented with the numbers, from one to nine, on a touch-screen monitor. The subject then had to remember which number appeared in which location.

[6] To make things harder, the team changed the task so that some numbers were missing. The subjects had to realize that if there was no number 3 for example, then 4 was the next number in the sequence after 2. The researchers made the experiment even tougher by steadily reducing the amount of time given to memorize the numbers and their position on the screen.

[7] When the team compared the chimps' performance with the student volunteers', they found the chimps left the humans standing. The difference was most noticeable when the chimps and students had very little time to memorize the numbers.

[8] Meanwhile in other studies, scientists are discovering that chimps sometimes behave more like humans than previously believed. Until recently, altruism – helping others for no reward – was considered a uniquely human characteristic. However, a German research team found that chimps will go out of their way to help others including chimps from outside their group and even other species.

[9] "We thought we were very different from other animals including our primate relatives, but this is not the case," Felix Warneken told The Sunday Times.

[10] In an experiment he conducted in Uganda, chimps saw a human volunteer trying unsuccessfully to reach for a stick. The chimps would pass the human the stick even when they had to climb over a 6ft(1.8m) wall to do so. The chimps did not know the humans and did not depend on them for food or favors, and they had not been trained or rewarded for performing this act of kindness.

[11] Helpful behavior is not uncommon in the animal world, but it is usually directed at members of the same species or pack where the survival of the group depends on the survival of each of its members. For an animal to help a member of a different species is far more surprising.

Word Work

7 Change the bold words in the sentence with a word chunk from the text.

a. When we visited my grandparents' village, I met someone who said he was a **fourth cousin** of mine.

_____

b. Although many **initially believed** that the earth was flat, this idea was proved wrong.

_____

c. **Studies carried out** by scientists show that primates have an amazing memory.

_____

d. My brother will **bend over backwards** to help someone, even a stranger.

_____

e. It's **not true** that I always prefer reading a book before I see the movie based on it.

is not the case.

8 Choose three chunks and make sentences about yourself or a friend.

a. _____

b. _____

c. _____

Who are the Most Intelligent?

Before Reading

1 Quickly skim the text. What is the text about? Check [✓] the best answer.

a. _____ The text explains why East Asians are more intelligent than people from English speaking countries.

b. _____ The text explains that there are forms of intelligence that are ignored by traditional ideas of intelligence.

c. _____ The text explains how scientific experiments can tell us which countries are more intelligent than others.

2 Quickly scan the text and underline names, dates, numbers, and pronouns. Then answer the following questions.

a. What does IQ stand for? _____

b. According to Professors Lyn and Vanhanen, which country has the highest intelligence, and where is the USA in their ranking? _____

c. Where was Isaac Asimov from? _____

While Reading

3 While you read the text, annotate it to help you remember significant ideas.

After Reading

4 Discuss the ideas you annotated with a partner.

5 Highlight the following:

a. the main idea of the text.

b. where each of the three supporting ideas starts.

6 Check [✓] the inferences you can make about the text. Underline the statements that help you make the inferences.

a. _____ A lot of people disagree with the ideas in Professors Lynn and Vanhanen's book, *IQ and The Wealth of Nations*.

b. _____ Dr. Asimov doesn't think IQ tests are a good measure of intelligence.

c. _____ Dr. Asimov doesn't think his car mechanic is very intelligent.

d. _____ The author thinks that car mechanics could be good science professors at university.

e. _____ Scoring highly in an American IQ test means you could be successful in any country including Bangladesh and Somalia.

Who are the Most Intelligent?

We all know people who are very intelligent and others who are not so intelligent, but can you explain why you think a friend, classmate, or colleague is intelligent? Is it because they did very
[5] well in school, or perhaps they know a lot about scientific and technological subjects? Maybe it is because they can speak different languages or because they can play a musical instrument very well.

There are tests designed to measure a person's
[10] IQ or intelligence quotient, and there is even an organization, MENSA, for people who score very highly in IQ tests and who are therefore thought to be the most intelligent people. But the truth is, it is difficult to find one definition of intelligence
[15] or a way of measuring intelligence that everyone can agree upon.

In their highly controversial book, 'IQ and the Wealth of Nations', Professors Richard Lynn and Tatu Vanhanen rank countries based on average
[20] national IQ, claiming that there is a strong link between the per capita wealth of a country and the intelligence of its population. Their top five most intelligent countries were Hong Kong, South Korea, Japan, Taiwan, and Singapore, with China
[25] coming in at number 13, the UK at number 15, Australia at 19, and the USA at 23. Does this mean that people from East Asian countries are more intelligent than people from English speaking countries?

[30] The famous Russian–born American scientist and writer, Isaac Asimov, who himself was a reluctant president of MENSA, questioned the definition of intelligence used as the basis of IQ tests. Asimov, a genius according to his scores in IQ tests, said
[35] in his autobiography that his high scores meant only that he was very good at answering the type of academic questions that are considered important by people who make up the intelligence tests – people who had the same or similar
[40] intellectual talents as him. These tests only measure one small aspect of intelligence.

In his book, Asimov includes a story about his car mechanic, a man who had a habit of telling jokes. One time the mechanic said to Asimov, "A deaf-
[45] and-mute guy went into a hardware store to ask for some nails. He put his thumb and first finger together as if he were holding a nail and made hammering motions with the other hand.

"The clerk brought him a hammer. The guy shook
[50] his head and pointed to the two fingers he was hammering. The clerk then brought him some nails and the guy picked out the sizes he wanted and left. Well, the next guy who came in was blind. He wanted scissors so how do you suppose
[55] he asked for them?"

Asimov, the genius, lifted his left hand and made motions like a pair of scissors with his first two fingers whereupon the mechanic laughed out loud and said, "Of course not you idiot. He used his
[60] voice, he just asked for them."

Then the mechanic said, "I've been trying that on all my customers today." "Did you catch many?" asked Asimov. "Quite a few," the mechanic replied, "but I knew for sure I'd catch you."

[65] "Why is that?" Asimov asked to which the mechanic replied, "Because you're so educated, doc, I knew you couldn't be very smart."

Who seems more intelligent in this situation? Dr. Asimov, the man with the higher IQ, or
[70] the mechanic?

IQ measures concentration, memory, verbal skills, and mathematical aptitude; forms of intelligence that are most valued in Western academic institutions. Indeed, the most successful people [75] in the U.S. tend to be those who concentrated in school, memorized information, and scored well on standardized tests. These are the people who get into the best colleges and eventually get the best jobs. We therefore come to see them [80] as intelligent.

But how useful are urban-American forms of "intelligence" in a Somalian village or rural Bangladesh? Having a large vocabulary or being good at math may not be the skills needed for [85] most people to be successful in those countries. The people who are considered intelligent in those countries may be the ones who simply know how to survive and provide for their families. This may require a set of skills that aren't measured by [90] current IQ tests such as: resilience, physical toughness, spatial awareness, and an ability to work well with people. If you placed a Harvard graduate in the middle of the Sahara with no food or water, he may not be "intelligent" enough to [95] survive.

So, which country or region contains the most intelligent people in the world? That depends on where you ask the question, and what questions you ask because the "intelligent" car mechanics [100] who can diagnose the problem with your car and repair it, may have nothing in common with the "intelligent" professors who teach science at the world's most prestigious universities. Multiple Intelligence theory suggests that schools, [105] universities, and employers would benefit from analyzing different intelligences rather than trying to judge an artificial overall intelligence with a single test. After all it would be better for a journalist to have strong interpersonal and linguistic [110] intelligences than mathematical and intrapersonal intelligences.

Word Work

7 | Make word chunks from the story, using the verbs in the box.

laugh	score	know how	provide	require

a. _____ to survive   b. _____ for their families
c. _____ out loud   d. _____ a set of skills
e. _____ well

8 | Choose three chunks and make sentences about yourself or a friend.
a. _____
b. _____
c. _____

Reflection

▶ Which was your favorite text in this unit? Why?

▶ Which reading strategies did you use in this unit?

▶ Which new word chunks will you make an effort to use in the next five days? Choose at least five.

Isn't It Romantic

Warm Up

1 Number the pictures 1 – 5. 1 is the most romantic and 5 the least romantic.

A

B

C

D

E

attitude

Reading Strategy: Understanding purpose and tone plus Separating fact from opinion

Purpose and Tone - Most texts aim to inform (describe or analyze), persuade (influence or convince), and / or entertain (amuse). Knowing the text's **purpose**—or why the writer has written the text—will help you understand what you are reading.

Identifying the text's **tone**—or the writer's attitude and feelings towards the subject of the text—will also help you understand what you are reading. The tone might be formal, informal, humorous, angry, enthusiastic, critical, etc. When reading, consider the words the writer chooses, the way he or she writes, and any opinions in the text.

Purpose and **tone** are closely linked. If the purpose of a text is to inform, the tone will usually be formal and objective. If the purpose is to persuade, the tone is more emotional; it might even be angry or enthusiastic. Entertaining texts are usually informal and emotional. A text with a formal or serious tone will include long sentences and have more sophisticated language, such as "provide" instead of "give," or "include" instead of "have" while an entertaining or informal text will include more exclamation marks (!), questions and opinions, and have more metaphors or slang, such as "she has a heart of gold", "he's a pain in the neck" or use the word "bucks" instead of "dollars" in American slang. *↳ she's nice*

Most texts may have more than one purpose and tone, so you should use your judgment to understand the writer's intention, attitude, and feelings.

Fact and Opinion - Writers often mix fact and opinion together in an argument, so it is important that the reader is able to understand the difference between them.

Facts are statements that everyone can agree are true, and can be proven. In a text, examples of facts are names, places, numbers, dates, and times.

Opinions on the other hand, are judgments or ideas and a reader may not have the same opinion as the writer.

Strategy in Focus

1 Read the text and decide its main purpose.

PARA informar   convencer

a. to inform   **b.** to persuade   **c.** to entertain PARA entretener

Best Movies of all Time
Casablanca (1942) – Best Romantic Movie

Casablanca is one of the greatest love stories ever told. It is as classic as it gets; black and white, set in Morocco, with a handsome leading man and a beautiful leading lady. Is this why it is so good?

Well no, it is not just because of Ingrid Bergman's heartbreaking gorgeousness, or Humphrey Bogart's soulful performance. Not even for *As Times Goes By*—a song that is so firmly linked to *Casablanca* that you want to say, "Play it again, Sam," each time you hear it. It is the story itself: An exiled, cynical American, Rick, owns a club in Casablanca, where he bumps into his old girlfriend, Ilsa. The story is also unique because of the romantic conflict. Set during World War II, Ilsa's husband is Resistance leader, Victor Lazslo, a noble guy with a heart of gold that both Rick and the audience cannot possibly dislike, which sets up an ending that is as romantic as it is sad. Rick sends Ilsa packing with a speech that punches you straight in the heart no matter how many times you watch it.

Like Humphrey Bogart, (a) **Casablanca is still cool after all these years**—(b) **the black and white cinematography is far more elegant than modern color**, and the dialog here is restrained and cynical, unlike the awkward monologues typical of so many films from the forties. But hey, if we think we are cynical now, just remember that (c) **this flick was shot in 1942**—times just do not get much worse than that.

2 The tone of this article is:

a. _____ serious   **b.** _____ informal   **c.** _____ humorous

3 Underline the parts of the text that indicate its tone.

4 Decide if the bold statements in the article are facts [F] or opinion [O].

a. O   **b.** O   **c.** F

Feedback

1. b. The main purpose of the text is to persuade. It is trying to convince the reader that Casablanca is the most romantic movie ever and probably trying to convince the reader to watch it.

2. and 3. b. The article is informal. It has a conversational style (asking and answering questions, for example) and uses informal language and expressions. Words such as, guy, hey and cool are considered informal as well as expressions such as, 'Rick sends Ilsa packing,' and 'punches you straight in the heart.'

4. a. O, b. O, c. F

A Long Lost Love

Before Reading

1 Skim the text and decide which of the following tones are used. Check [✓] your answers.

a. _____ serious **b.** _____ critical **c.** _____ inspirational **d.** _____ optimistic

e. _____ formal **f.** _____ sad **g.** _____ informal **h.** _____ angry

2 What is the purpose of the text?

a. a newspaper article to persuade the readers that you can only love one person.

b. an academic text to inform the reader about Russian history.

c. a story to inspire the reader to believe in the lasting power of love.

While Reading

3 Decide if you are correct about the text's purpose and tone.

After Reading

4 Associate the text with your personal experiences. Tell a partner:

a. how you felt after reading the text.

b. about people you know who have fallen in love.

c. if you believe in love at first sight.

5 Decide if you agree [✓] or disagree [✓] with these judgments.

a. _____ Anna's mother was wrong to burn the letters, poems, and pictures.

b. _____ Internal exile is not as bad as going to prison.

c. _____ Anna and Boris are too old to have gotten married again in their eighties.

d. _____ This is one of the sweetest love stories I have ever read.

6 Decide if the bold statements in the text are fact (F) or opinion (O).

a. _____ **b.** _____ **c.** _____ **d.** _____ **e.** _____ **f.** _____

7 Decide if the statements are true (T) or false (F), according to the text.

a. T (F) Anna grew up in a large city.

b. T (F) Boris and Anna had a fancy wedding in 1946.

c. (T) F Both Anna and Boris remarried when they could not find each other.

d. T (F) Boris and Anna were both living in the same village when they saw each other in 2006.

A Long Lost Love

Boris and Anna Kozlov have a classic love story. Like many young people in love, they only had eyes for each other when they met. He was a handsome young soldier, she was a

[5] beautiful village girl and she caught his eye. (a.) **He thought she was the most beautiful girl around**. They quickly fell for each other and despite sharing different political views —— (b.) **Boris was a soldier in Stalin's Red Army**, while

[10] most of Anna's family were outspoken critics of the regime —— they were in love and nothing else seemed to matter. Even though Boris had to go back to fight at the front, they knew they would marry.

[15] When the fighting was over and Boris returned, the country was in ruins and the couple had little money for an elaborate wedding, but that did not matter. Boris and Anna were in love and just eager to settle down together. (c.) **They were married**

[20] **in 1946**; however three days into their marriage, Boris had to rejoin his army unit. "We kissed goodbye, but I never expected we wouldn't see each other for more than half a century," Anna said.

[25] While Boris was away, Anna and her family were accused of being enemies of the state and they were forced to live as exiles in Siberia. By the time Boris again returned to the village, Anna was gone and no one knew where she now lived.

[30] Boris desperately searched for her but could not find his young wife.

Meanwhile in Siberia, Anna was broken hearted. Her mother was desperate for her daughter to move on with her life and burned all of Boris'

[35] photos, poems, and love letters, thinking that this would help. It did not, and as Anna said, (d.) **"It was the most miserable time of my life."** Finally, convinced that she would never see Boris again, Anna reluctantly agreed to remarry, as did

[40] Boris. Yet they never forgot each other, their first true loves.

Boris went on to become a writer and dedicated a book to the woman he had married as a young soldier, hoping that perhaps Anna would see it,

[45] though she never did. When the Soviet Union dissolved, Anna was once again permitted to travel and she moved back to her home village. It was there that Anna caught sight of an elderly man climbing out of a car.

[50] "I thought my eyes were playing games with me," Anna said. "I saw this familiar-looking man approaching me, his eyes gazing at me. My heart jumped. I knew it was him. I was crying with joy."

Boris had been visiting the village to pay respects

[55] at his parents' grave when he noticed a woman standing in front of the house that he and his wife had lived in for those three brief days sixty years before. He was sure it was her and quickly went over to her, saying, "Darling, I've been waiting for

[60] you for so long." They stayed up all night talking about what had happened over the years. They realized that they were still head over heels in love.

Both were widowed and Boris was anxious to

[65] marry again, although Anna was a little hesitant. (e.) **She thought she was too old to be a bride again**. However, Boris was persuasive and Anna gave in, and is glad she did for as she said, "It was my happiest wedding."

[70] "I couldn't take my eyes off her. (f.) **Yes, I had loved other women when we were separated**, but she was the true love of my life." Although Boris and Anna missed out on sixty years together, they are determined to cherish every minute of

[75] what is left.

Word Work

8 | Match the word chunk with its definition.

a. catch someone's eye   i. be very much in love with someone
b. fall for someone   ii. be devastated; very sad
c. settle down   iii. fall in love
d. be broken hearted   iv. find someone attractive
e. be head over heels in love   v. live together

9 | Choose three chunks and make sentences about yourself or a friend.

a. Yestarday, I saw a hundsome main who caught my eye.
b. Have you ever fallen in love?
c. couples usually settle down after having children.

Homework

Reading 2 The Science of Attraction

Before Reading

1 Look at the title and the picture then skim the first paragraph of the text. What is the purpose of the text? *pers-veide* ~~persuade~~

a. To persuade the reader that romantic love does not exist.
b. To inform the reader of how science can explain why we pick certain partners. *(circled)*
c. To explain the physical effects of falling in love.

While Reading

2 While you read the text, annotate it to help you remember significant ideas.

After Reading

3 What do you think of the text? Check [✓] your answers. The text is:

a. _____ funny. b. ✓ surprising. c. _____ boring. d. ✓ interesting. e. _____ sad.

4 Complete the outline of the text.

The Science of Attraction
i. Evolutionary theory explains a person's choice in partner.
ii. visual: _____
iii. _____ low voice = more attractive
iv. olfactory: _____
v. _____ : allows for the amplification of other senses.
vi. neurochemical: dopamine, _____ , _____ .

5 Decide if the bold statements in the text are fact (F) or opinion (O) according to the text.

a. _____   b. _____   c. _____   d. _____   e. _____   f. _____

6 Decide if you agree [✓] or disagree [×] with the interpretations of these sentences.

	Interpretation	✓ / ×
a. " ... men look for women with symmetrical faces, which indicates a strong genetic make-up ..." (line 21)	Men are looking for women who wear a lot of make-up.	✓
b. " ... but this <u>tactile experience</u> allows for an amplification of other information ..." (line 69)	When people kiss, everything seems louder and smells stronger.	×
c. "Dopamine creates a feeling of happiness, similar to the effects of caffeine ..." (line 87)	Because of the release of dopamine, being in love can be as addictive as a drug.	✓

CD 1:
Track 4

The Science of Attraction

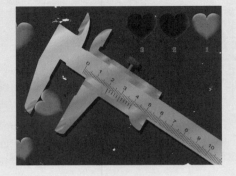

beard *Kind*

We see someone we are attracted to across a room and our eyes lock on them. Our heart starts beating faster, our hands get sweaty, we start blushing, and we forget about everything else. [5] Love has struck, but why? It may be unromantic, but it turns out that falling in love follows a complex combination of positive visual, auditory, olfactory, tactile, and neurochemical processes.

The science of attraction, or the way that we [10] pick partners, can be explained by evolutionary theory. (a.) **Evolutionary scientists believe that humans are hardwired to look for a mate with the best possible genes which will be passed on to future, healthy offspring**. However, how [15] can someone determine if a potential partner's genes are desirable?

Traits pista

The most obvious clue to this is the visual assessment – checking out the person's appearance. Visually, people look for certain [20] physical traits in the opposite sex. For instance, some studies suggest that men look for women with symmetrical faces, which indicates a strong genetic make-up, and a low waist-to-hip measurement and large chest which may [25] be signs of fertility. Women, on the other hand, unconsciously look for signs of virility and strength such as muscular shoulders, a broad chest, and full beard. (b.) **The belief is that men with these features will be better able to father children** [30] **and protect the family from future danger**.

The second thing we unconsciously take into account deals with the auditory process – a person's voice. David Feinberg of McMaster University in Ontario studied Tanzania's Hadza [35] tribe and found that men who had a lower and richer voice had more children. Another study from the University of Albany found that those

people whose voice was rated 'very attractive' by a group of volunteers usually also had physical [40] features that were considered more sexually appealing, such as men with broad shoulders and women with a low waist-to-hip ratio.

consciente

While people might be conscious of how appearance and voice can spark attraction, many [45] might not be aware of how olfactory processes also quietly influence their choice of mate. The importance of the sense of smell is not just connected to someone's choice of cologne or perfume; instead it also refers to very subtle [50] odorless chemicals called pheromones which are present in sweat and saliva.

A study by the University of Bern in Switzerland asked women to smell T-shirts worn by anonymous males and then pick the one that most appealed [55] to them. (c.) **Over and over, the women chose shirts worn by men who had different immune systems to them**. Having a different immune system could result in any future offspring developing a stronger combined immune system, [60] giving them a reduced risk of early death. But how does someone detect if another's immune system is different? The answer is, sample the other person's major histocompatibility complex (MHC), a pheromone that can be detected in [65] sweat, as well as saliva. (d.) **Some speculate that the custom of kissing might be simply explained as figuring out if someone's MHC is different from your own**.

Kissing not only carries pheromones, but this [70] tactile experience also allows for an amplification of other information, such as scent, sound, and physical information. (e.) **In addition, kissing is a way men pass on trace amounts of testosterone**. There is a possibility therefore that

[75] kissing evolved as one way that men could pass on a natural chemical that would attract women to them.

It is the neurochemical processes, or what occurs in the brain, that makes love feel so good. [80] Pictures taken of brains of people in love show that the "feeling of being in love" is processed in three areas and vary in intensity depending on how long the person has been in love.

For people newly in love, (f.) **the part of the** [85] **brain that responds most strongly is the ventral tegmental, which is the body's central repository for dopamine**. Dopamine creates a feeling of happiness, similar to the effects of caffeine, which is intoxicating and exhilarating. [90] This stage of attraction is usually referred to as 'lust.' However, too much dopamine could be overwhelming and could lead to obsession, so eventually the body passes those feelings on to the brain's nucleus accumbens. Here, serotonin

[95] and oxytocin help turn those obsessive feelings into attachment. When two partners are close, oxytocin is released, which is responsible for creating a strong emotional bond. The third area of the brain processing these feelings is the [100] caudate nuclei, the area responsible for forming habits and patterns. Once these feelings are processed here love becomes a familiar habit that most people do not want to break.

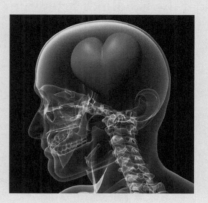

Word Work

7 Complete the sentences with a word chunk from the text.

physical traits	the opposite sex	take into account	sense of smell
immune system	risk death	trace amounts	

a. Because Fred had a weak <u>immune system</u>; he often got sick.

b. Before you get angry with Angie for forgetting your birthday, you should <u>take into account</u> that her mother has been sick and is in hospital.

c. When you travel overseas, be careful of drinking tap water because it may contain <u>trace amounts</u> of bacteria that will make you sick.

d. I have no <u>sense of smell</u> and as a result, I have no sense of taste either.

8 Choose three chunks and make sentences about yourself or a friend.

a. _____

b. _____

c. _____

Reflection

▶ Which was your favorite text in this unit? Why?

▶ Which reading strategies did you use in this unit?

▶ Which new word chunks will you make an effort to use in the next five days? Choose at least five.

3 Two Sides to the Story

Warm Up

1 **Look at the headlines below and tell a partner:**
   a. what the stories are about.
   b. if each story will be positive or negative.

"Brave Fire Fighter Rescues Girl from Blazing Inferno",

"Out of Control Celebrity in Trouble with Police" .

2 **Rewrite the headlines so they are neither positive nor negative.**

Reading Strategy: Recognizing bias

All writers have a point of view or preference which can affect how they tell a story, describe a situation, or provide information. The writer will often present the story or situation in a way that reflects his or her opinion. This is called **bias**.

Sometimes writers know they are expressing their **bias** and sometimes it is unintentional.

By **recognizing bias** you can form your own opinions and make your own judgments. Recognizing a writer's bias will also help you judge how much you agree with the text.

Examples of bias are found in:

- **Headlines / Titles** The first headline about the fire fighter is an example of positive bias. The second headline is an example of negative bias. By using the words "Out of Control" the writer implies the actor is crazy. An unbiased headline may be, "Actor Questioned by Police."
- **Photos** The close-up of a tired-and-angry-looking person out of context may influence you to think this person is unreasonable.

Bias takes these forms:

- **Exaggeration / Sensationalism / Distortion**
  Sensational words can strongly influence the reader. For example, "Brave Fire Fighter Rescues Girl from Blazing Inferno," is much more exciting than, "Fireman Helps Woman Escape Kitchen Fire."
  Statistics and numbers can also make a news story seem more spectacular or interesting. For example, "Hundreds injured in air crash," is more sensational than, "Airline passengers sustain minor injuries in accident."
- **Imbalance / Omission / Over Simplification**
  A writer also shows bias by presenting one side of an argument or one opinion fully and only producing a short amount of text on other points of view.

Strategy in Focus

1 | Check [✓]the types of bias shown in the text below.

   a. _____ headline bias   **b.** _____ photo bias   **c.** _____ imbalance bias
   d. _____ word choice bias   **e.** _____ statistics and numbers bias

The Tragedy

The great, powerful, and fearsome polar bear is helpless in the face of global warming. If the current distressing trends continue, the Arctic will be ice-free in summer by 2040, robbing polar bears of all they need to survive.

A SERIOUS PROBLEM

Global warming is causing the Arctic sea ice to melt at an alarming rate, threatening the very existence of polar bears and other wildlife. The last two years saw the greatest loss of sea ice ever recorded. During the 20th century, air temperatures in some parts of the Arctic rose by a staggering 5° C (9° F) – ten times faster than the global average. Furthermore, scientists predict that world temperatures could continue to rise by an incredible 6° C (10.5° F) by 2100.

In the Arctic, ice thickness has already declined by over 40 percent, and an area of ice larger than the Netherlands is disappearing every year.

YOU CAN HELP

Stop this madness by joining the thousands of students expected to march in protest of the devastating rise in global warming. We must send a loud and clear message to the government.

Meet outside the main library on Thursday at 10 a.m. to join the march.

2 | Underline and rewrite the biased phrase in each sentence so it is neutral.

   a. The great, powerful and fearsome polar bear is helpless in the face of global warming.

   _____

   b. If the current distressing trends continue, the Arctic will be ice-free in summer by 2040, robbing polar bears of all they need to survive.

   _____

   c. Stop this madness by joining the thousands of students expected to march in protest of the devastating rise in global warming.

   _____

3 | Underline other phrases in the text that show a bias.

Feedback

1. a, b, c, d, e
2. a. great, powerful and fearsome polar bear -The Polar bear b. current distressing - If the trends continue
   c. Stop this madness... thousands - Join the march in protest ...
3. THE TRAGEDY; A SERIOUS PROBLEM, at an alarming rate; threatening the very existence; rose by a staggering; an incredible 6° C, scientists predict that ...

All of these examples of bias use sensational language or exaggerated language, except the "scientists predict ..." which is an example of an omission as it would be more accurate if it reads "some scientists predict ..." The text is also imbalanced because it only presents one side of the argument.

Is it Wrong to Save an Orphan?

Before Reading

1 | Tell a partner what you know about Madonna and what you know about adoption.

beautiful gesture + gescher

2 | Skim the text and decide its purpose.

a. to inform the reader that Madonna has adopted a baby from Africa.

(b.) to persuade the readers that international adoption is a good idea.

c. to entertain the reader with a story about the pop star, Madonna.

persveide

While Reading

3 | As you read the news story, consider the bias and decide if you agree [✓] or disagree [×] with the interpretations of the underlined words.

	Interpretation	✓ / ×
a. "Madonna's adoption of a little boy from Malawi is a perfect example of this <u>blind criticism</u>." (line 10)	The people who are criticizing Madonna do not have facts to support their ideas.	✓
b. "They also established a fund <u>guaranteeing the future</u> of the orphanage. (line 15)	Gave the orphanage money to help feed, house and educate children for a long time in the future.	✓
c. "Yohane, David's father and a single parent, had already <u>lost his wife</u>" (line 21)	David's father cannot remember where his wife lives.	×
d. "David will <u>enjoy advantages</u> he could never receive otherwise." (line 39)	David will have money, a nice house, good clothes, and an excellent education.	✓

After Reading

4 | Check [✓] the type of biases shown in the text.

a. _____ headline   b. ✓ photo   c. ✓ imbalance

d. _____ word choice   e. _____ statistic and numbers

5 | Complete the sentences from the first paragraph, using a reference word from the box. Do not look at the text.

such   who   this   some

In a time of so much suffering from poverty, war and disease, it is amazing that people _who_ try to help others are publicly criticized. International adoption has suffered from _such_ criticism in recent years. In America and Western Europe, families have been helping less advantaged people in Africa, Asia and Eastern Europe for decades, yet there are _some_ who claim that international adoption is wrong no matter what the reasons and circumstances. Madonna's adoption of a little boy from Malawi is a perfect example of _this_ blind criticism.

Is it Wrong to Save an Orphan?

In a time of so much suffering from poverty, war, and disease, it is amazing that people who try to help others are publicly criticized. International adoption has suffered from such criticism in
[5] recent years. In America and Western Europe, families have been adopting children to help less advantaged people in Africa, Asia, and Eastern Europe for decades yet there are some who claim that international adoption is wrong no matter
[10] what the reasons and circumstances. Madonna's adoption of a little boy from Malawi is a perfect example of this blind criticism.

A few years ago the American singer and her British husband rescued a baby from life in a
[15] Malawi orphanage and a future of poverty. They also established a fund guaranteeing the future of the orphanage. Even this did not stop some hard-line activists protesting Madonna's adoption of David Banda saying it was an abuse of the
[20] boy's human rights.

Yohane, David's father and a single parent, had already lost his wife and two children when he made the tough decision to take David to the orphanage.
[25] He was deeply concerned about his son's health and welfare as his other children had died of malaria, and he was also worried about his own ability to raise David without his wife. "I was alone with a baby. I had no money, I couldn't buy him milk; that's why I surrendered him to the
[30] orphanage," Banda told a reporter. "Orphanage life is not good. We only leave kids there because we cannot look after them properly ourselves. Now my son has been taken by a kindhearted woman. These people [who protest the adoption]
[35] want to bring him back to the orphanage."

Yohane believes David will lead a better life in the West, where he will have every opportunity to succeed, especially being the child of a pop star. David will enjoy advantages he could never
[40] receive otherwise. Surely denying David this opportunity would be a bigger abuse of his and his father's human rights.

As well as helping the orphanage and David, Madonna and her husband gave the government
[45] a generous $3 million donation to help children in Malawi infected with HIV. They are also funding the Raising Malawi center to feed and educate Aids orphans in Mphandula. Mphandula is a village of mud huts with thatched roofs, no mains
[50] electricity, and only a handful of radios, where few would have heard Madonna's music. Many households there are headed by children who have lost parents to Aids and are left to raise their siblings. Of Malawi's population of 13 million,
[55] about one million are children who have lost at least one parent.

Despite Madonna's obviously good intentions, her critics claimed that the Malawi government broke its own rules on adoption. Normally, prospective
[60] parents have to stay in the country for 18 months while being evaluated before they are allowed to adopt. The law is meant to discourage foreign adoption.

When asked about this matter at the time,
[65] Madonna's spokesperson said in a statement, "Madonna and her husband's plan to adopt a child from Malawi has been in the works for several months. Being granted the adoption was the first step in the legal process to bring the baby
[70] to England."

continued on page 28

Some criticize international or inter-country adoption altogether. They say that inter-country adoption removes the children from the culture into which they are born, and that babies are [75] being bought and sold like a commodity. Some extremists have even gone so far as to suggest that international adoption encourages child trafficking (stealing or buying children from their parents to sell at a higher price to rich couples) and even link [80] it to slavery or forced military service.

However, what these alarmists fail to consider is that, in most cases, international adoption results in a child being raised within the nurturing environment of a family instead of an under- [85] resourced institution such as an orphanage. Economically, a child almost always steps up into a higher class and the child is given new educational opportunities.

[90] There are estimates of between 50 and 200 million orphans in the world today. These are some of the most vulnerable children of the world. They have been abandoned by their parents, often because of poverty or sickness, and as a result, tens of millions of children will grow up without a [95] loving family to care for them. This is contrary to the United Nations Convention on the Rights of the Child, which states that it is better for children to grow up in a family environment. However, finding homes and families for these children is [100] increasingly difficult.

If more people follow in the footsteps of Madonna and others like Hollywood actress Angelina Jolie, who has adopted children from Cambodia and Ethiopia, there would be fewer children suffering [105] on their own and without the protection of a loving family.

Word Work

6 Write sentences about the text using these word chunks.

... be deeply concerned ...
... lead a better life ...
... good intentions ...
... break its own rules ...
... be in the works ...
... educational opportunities ...
... abandoned by their parents ...
... grow up in a family environment ...

7 Choose three chunks and make sentences about yourself or a friend.

a. _____

b. _____

c. _____

I came to America to lead a better life when I was 4 years old

The Business of Adoption

Before Reading

1 Quickly skim the text and highlight the main ideas.

2 Quickly scan the text to find names, dates, numbers, and pronouns. Answer the questions.
  a. Where was Tristan born?
  b. Where were his adopted parents from?
  c. How long did Tristan live with his adopted parents?
  d. How many children adopted from other countries live in Ireland?
  e. How many children were adopted to families in other countries in 2006?

While Reading

3 While you read the text, note the bias and make annotations to help you remember significant ideas.

After Reading

4 The tone of this article is:
  a. humorous.   **b.** conversational.   **c.** critical

5 Underline the parts of the text that indicate its tone.

6 Check [✓] the types of bias shown in the text.
  a. _____ headline   **b.** _____ photo   **c.** _____ imbalance   **d.** _____ word choice
  e. _____ statistics and numbers

7 Underline phrases in the text that show a bias.

8 Decide if the bold statements in the text are fact (F) or opinion (O) according to the article.
  a. _____   **b.** _____   **c.** _____   **d.** _____   **e.** _____

CD 1:
Track 6

The Business of Adoption

Tristan, a young Indonesian boy (a.) **was just two months old when he was adopted** by an Irish man and his Azerbaijani wife who were then living in Indonesia. Sadly, they felt unable to bond
[5] with him and just two years later, he was once again taken in by an Indonesian orphanage.

By the time he was abandoned, his parents who were not expecting to remain in Indonesia, had arranged for Tristan to obtain an Irish passport. His
[10] new nationality created additional complications for the poor toddler and Tristan was threatened with being sent to Ireland even though he had no family or friends there. Fortunately, (b.) **his heartbreaking story touched many in Ireland**
[15] and led to a documentary film for an Irish TV company, *The Search for Tristan's Mum*.

While the documentary recorded the successful search for Tristan's natural mother it also highlighted some of the problems that come
[20] with inter-country adoptions and examined the booming international adoption business.

International adoptions that we normally read about tend to feature a hopeless, unwanted, or abandoned child who is rescued from an unhappy
[25] life in a developing country. There are currently more than 3,000 of these "rescued" children living in Ireland. (c.) **The rate of international adoptions to Ireland each year leapt from just four in 1991 to almost 500 in recent years**,
[30] all too many of them babies from developing countries. And across the globe, that pattern is being replicated; (d.) **in 2006, 40,000 children were adopted from poor countries by western couples.**

[35] (e.) **International adoptions are usually described as a win-win situation for the couples and the children**, but at the root of many international adoptions, (f.) **there is a story of a lucrative business that is open to abuse.**

[40] Most people who adopt do not realize or simply close their eyes to this. Some might have their suspicions but these are brushed aside in the emotion of adopting a child.

In the heartwarming stories of adoptions, money
[45] is rarely talked about and even if it is mentioned, the amounts would seem reasonable by western standards. However in the developing countries where the children are taken from, it can be a fortune, and the motivation provided by a large
[50] sum of money means that when Westerners go abroad looking for a child, they get what they want. (g.) **Without the money as motivation to find orphans, these children may not be given up to orphanages and then on to families half
[55] way around the world.**

Asian countries are becoming popular adoption locations. The adoption process may only cost around $7000 in some countries, but in some areas adoptions are only handled by one agency
[60] so couples sometimes feel held to ransom.

Remarkably, the first half of the fee may often be paid by bankers' draft made payable not to the local government or social services, but directly to the individual running the adoption agency. Even
[65] more ominously, the adopters are then required to bring the second part of the fee in cash. When the average salary is maybe around $240 a year, the question of why it takes such sums of money for even a government endorsed adoption leads
[70] to suggestions of corruption.

The money that adopters bring to economically poor countries means that they get the babies

continued on page 31

they want regardless of the rights of the natural parents or other ethical considerations. The [75] money means there will always be a ready supply of babies and according to some U.S. childcare experts, vulnerable women are being preyed upon.

One report from the U.S. Embassy in Romania [80] stated, "... children are being adopted out of Romania who would not, in the absence of the financial incentive, have been placed for adoption at all, let alone adopted internationally."

Irish parents who have adopted children may point [85] to the shocking conditions in the orphanages and say the children would have remained there if they had not been adopted. However some time ago, the head of the EU delegation in Bucharest, reported that inter-country adoption, far from [90] being an answer to over-crowded orphanages, is in fact the reason some orphanages exist at all.

He called Romanian orphanages little more than warehouses full of children for sale. "The desirability of having what is in practice a stock of [95] children suitable for adoption, means you do not really want to encourage too much contact with the natural parents because that might make the child less easy to move into adoption," he said.

It is clear that as long as there is money involved, [100] inter-country adoptions will not serve to properly help poor families who are struggling to survive. The money will instead create incentives to "sell" children who are not necessarily true orphans and increase the speed of the adoptions to families [105] who might not be fit to adopt.

Based, with permission, on an article by Phelim McAleer.

Word Work

9 Circle the correct word chunk.

a. I think that working while going to school is a **win-win situation** / **a win-win state** because I can get workplace experience and also make money to help pay for school.
b. Many people **shuttered their eyes** / **closed their eyes** to the genocide that occurred in Rwanda during the 1990s.
c. I heard **a heartburning story** / **a heartwarming story** of a young girl who gave her weekly allowance to the homeless.
d. The **shocking conditions** / **shocking surroundings** of the country's prison system prompted many human rights organizations to speak out.
e. After spending seven days lost in the desert, it was **a fight to survive** / **a struggle to survive** because I was running out of water.

10 Choose three chunks and make sentences about yourself or a friend.
a. _____
b. In my country most of people closed their eyes for the goverment
c. In my re _____

Reflection

▶ Which was your favorite text in this unit? Why?

▶ Which reading strategies did you use in this unit?

▶ Which new word chunks will you make an effort to use in the next five days? Choose at least five.

Review Reading Strategies

- Unit 1: Highlighting and annotating
- Unit 2: Understanding purpose and tone; separating fact from opinion
- Unit 3: Recognizing bias

→ Fillings   *→ preference*

1 Which of the reading strategies do these sentences describe? Write highlight, annotate, purpose, tone, fact, opinion, or bias next to the sentence.

	Reading Strategy
a. A statement expressing an attitude about something.	*Opinion*
b. Write brief notes in the margins of a text.	*annotate*
c. If you describe a text as funny, serious, critical, or informal, what are you descrbing?	*Tone*
d. Draw attention to a main idea or useful information with color.	*highlight*
e. A statement expressing something that has happened and it can be proved.	*Fact*
f. Noting down your thoughts, opinions, questions about a reading.	*annotate*
g. An author's point of view which may affect how they tell a story	*bias*
h. The reason an author has written a text for example, to persuade, inform, or entertain.	*purpose*
i. Exaggeration, sensationalism, imbalance, omission, and over simplification are forms of this.	*bias*

2 Read the second paragraph of the text. What is the main idea?

a. to entertain the reader with a story about two people named Martin and Sherchan.
b. to persuade people to give up unhealthy habits and live healthier.
c. to explain what people are doing to extend and improve the quality of their lives.

3 Decide the tone of the text.

a. informal and serious   b. informal and enthusiastic   c. informal and humorous

Homework

4 Match the annotation to the paragraph.

Annotation	Paragraph
a. Daily physical activity is vital to longevity.	1 / 2 / 3 / 4 / 5 / 6
b. Life expectancy is increasing.	1 / 2 / 3 / 4 / 5 / 6
c. Are these stories true? Unbelievable!	1 / 2 / 3 / 4 / 5 / 6
d. Important to take time to relax.	1 / 2 / 3 / 4 / 5 / 6
e. Blue zones: Europe, Asia, North and Central America.	1 / 2 / 3 / 4 / 5 / 6

Living Long and Prospering

[1] At 101 years old, Buster Martin became the world's oldest marathon runner. The former army physical training officer took approximately 10 hours to finish the 26.2-mile (42 km) London Marathon in April 2008. A month later, over 2,000 miles away on the highest peak in the world, Min Bahadur Sherchan climbed Mt. Everest, just 25 days shy of his 77th birthday. At an age when most people are content to stay at home and enjoy their retirement, these two men accomplished physical feats that people much younger than them do not even dream about. Have they discovered the elusive fountain of youth?

[2] As life expectancy increases, stories like Martin and Sherchan's will become more and more common. Although the magical fountain of youth has yet to be discovered, people are becoming more aware of how to live longer, healthier lives. Dan Buettner has researched what he considers to be the keys to longevity in his book, *The Blue Zones: Lessons for Living Longer from the People Who've Lived the Longest.*

[3] Buettner traveled the world and identified four places, which he calls blue zones, where people seem to have a three times better chance to reach 100 than people elsewhere. The Italian island of Sardinia has the highest number of male centenarians in the world, while another island, Okinawa, Japan, has the longest disability-free life expectancy. In Loma Linda, California, a small community has a life expectancy that's nine to 11 years greater than that of other people in the US. And middle-age mortality is lowest on Costa Rica's Nicoya Peninsula.

[4] Scientists agree that genetics plays less than a 25 percent part in the aging process, and Buettner noticed some similarities between those people who lived in the blue zones, which may help to increase life expectancy. First of all, their living environment encouraged physical activity. For example, Costa Ricans are more likely to have gardens, Sardinians live in vertical houses, and Okinawans sit on the floor, all of which encourage movement. Buettner also noticed that their kitchens were set up in a certain way that did not encourage overeating. For example, the plate size of the Okinawans is considerably smaller than those of say the average American family. People in the blue zones also have a sense of purpose and surround themselves with a good support group, be it friends or family. All of these are life-long habits not temporary changes, a fact that seems to contribute to a longer and better quality of life.

[5] If you are not lucky enough to already live in one of these blue zones, Buettner suggests incorporating some of the following practices in your own life to enjoy similar benefits. He believes that people have much more control over how long they live than they might have previously thought. Scientists agree that about 75 percent of longevity is dictated by how we live, and with the right lifestyle changes, experts believe that people can live up to a decade longer. For one, make your home less convenient. Instead of relying on a remote control, get up and change the channels manually. If you have children, get out and play with them; it will provide exercise and will help strengthen personal connections. Try to relax for an hour a day with a nap, meditation, or a quiet walk, anything to help de-stress as this could slow the aging process. Eat tofu and nuts – both contain important ingredients that will strengthen your immune system and improve your health. Finally, set yourself a personal mission – take into account what you want to do and how you can do it. Do you want to settle down and have a family, travel around the world, or volunteer your time? Knowing what you want will give you a sense of purpose and can help prolong your life.

[6] Although old-age seems a long way off and you might not want to run a marathon or scale Mount Everest when you are old and gray, no one wants to suffer later in life, and making some small changes now will help you lead a better life throughout the ages.

Comprehension Check

Homework

1 Decide if the statements are true (T) or false (F), according to the article.

a. T **(F)** Genetics plays the major role in how long someone lives.

b. **(T)** F A little bit of physical activity and eating in moderation can help prolong your life.

c. T F Min Bahadur Sherchan was 76 when he climbed Mt. Everest.

d. T **(F)** Making some small lifestyle changes can add 10 years to your life.

2 The word "feats" in paragraph one is closest in meaning to:

a. exercises   b. activities   c. challenges   d. accomplishments → *realizações*

3 Which of the following is NOT a lifestyle change mentioned in the text?

a. know what you want to do.   **b.** get plenty of sleep

c. eat smaller amounts of food   d. engage in physical activity

4 The word "centenarians" in paragraph 3 is closest in meaning to:

a. very active people.   **b.** people who are over 100.

c. people who are healthy.   d. people living in Sardinia.

5 Check [✓] the inferences you can make about the text. Underline the words, phrases, or sentences that support your inferences.

a. _____ Martin and Sherchan are in good cardiovascular shape.

b. _____ The elderly of Okinawa probably do not have to take a lot of medication or receive a lot of physical therapy.

c. _____ Sardinians get some of their exercise from walking up and down stairs.

d. _____ People do not have much control over their own longevity.

e. _____ Remote controls and other labor-saving devices are not necessarily good for your health.

f. _____ Stress can be controlled through exercise or meditation.

More Word Chunks

1 Complete the word chunks.

thought	settle	immune	account	lead

a. Because I am only twenty, I have never given much thought to how I could _____ a better life.

b. I had previously _____ that I would not need to worry about my health until I was much older.

c. But as I see my parents age, I am beginning to take into _____ what I can do now to improve my health later.

d. For example, I used to eat a lot of fast food, but now, to improve my _____ system I eat much more fruit and vegetables.

e. Although I am not ready to _____ down, I do plan on spending a lot of quality time with my friends and family.

Homework

2 Write sentences about yourself or someone you know using word chunks from Units 1, 2, and 3.

a. go out of the way: _I am going to work but I am going out of the my_
b. laugh out loud: _Yesterday I saw a movie that we made me way laugh out loud_
c. fall for someone: _____
d. educational opportunities: _____
e. a win-win situation: _____

3 In Units 1 and 3 we learned about the word chunk "to provide for their families" and "grow up in a family environment."

> 'Deadbeat dads' is the term used to describe fathers who leave their children and do not **provide for their families.**
> I was lucky to **grow up in a family environment** with a mother and a father who loved me.

Here are some other word chunks with "family" and their definitions:

> immediate family (the closest relations)
> nuclear family (parents and children)
> raise a family (bring up)
> a family man (a man who is devoted to his wife and kids)
> single parent family (a family consisting of one parent who is raising the children)
> runs in the family (similar characteristics that family members may share)
> a family history (pertaining to medical records – what illnesses affected family members)

Complete the sentences with a word chunk from the box above.

a. My father has always been _____ and spends all his free time doting on my mother and my siblings and me.
b. My parents got divorced when I was three and my father moved to another country. So essentially for the past fourteen years, I have been in a _____.
c. Athleticism is something that _____ as my parents and my grandparents were very good at sports.
d. For my graduation party, I am only inviting my _____, not my second and third cousins.
e. When you see a doctor, he or she will ask you about your _____ so make sure you know about any medical conditions that your parents or grandparents had.

4 Money Makers

Warm Up

Take the millionaire quiz and score your answers. Do you have potential to become a millionaire?

1 **How much sleep do you like a night?**
   a. 6 hours or less
   b. 8 hours
   c. 12 hours

3 **You win $10,000 in a competition. Do you**
   a. invest it?
   b. go on a great vacation?
   c. spend it on an unforgettable party?

5 **What is your attitude when playing sports?**
   a. I always try to win.
   b. It does not matter if you win or lose; it is how you play the game.
   c. I think competition is bad for your mental health

2 **Do you**
   a. find it easy to concentrate on things you are interested in?
   b. sometimes get distracted?
   c. find it difficult to concentrate?

4 **Which of the following motivates you the most?**
   a. interesting work
   b. deadlines
   c. praise

6 **Where do you buy your clothes?**
   a. chain stores
   b. designer boutiques
   c. I make my own.

Give yourself 3 points for every a, 2 points for every b and 1 point for every c.
13–18 points: millionaire attitude: financially careful, hard-working and dedicated to a success.
7–12 points: millionaire potential: become a better money manager and devote time to success.
1–6 points: no millionaire potential: enjoy your life!

Reading Strategy: Reading fluency

Fluency is the ability to read a text without stopping.
In order to become a more **fluent** reader:
- **Read every day.** Students who read every day will become more fluent readers.
- **Use** previewing strategies before you start reading, such as hypothesizing, skimming, and scanning. Look at titles and pictures and ask yourself what you think you are going to read about.
- **Think in English.** Do not translate English words into your first language. Understand the main ideas, and do not worry about trying to understand every word.
- **Read in chunks** rather than word by word. Look for common collocations that go together.
- **Do not pronounce each word** as you read. Our brains and eyes work much faster than speech.
- **Keep reading.** Re-read if necessary, but do not stop to understand every difficult word or idea.

Strategy in Focus

1 You will have one minute to read the following text. Stop when the teacher tells you to and make a mark after the last word you have read.

The Farmer's Daughter And Her Bucket

A farmer's daughter was once walking down the dirt road to the market with a full bucket of milk on her head. She swayed this way and that. The milk danced about the inside of the bucket, but not a drop dripped over.

Suddenly she tripped on a small stone in the path and stumbled, almost dropping the bucket. "Oh, I must be careful not to spill the milk!" the girl said to herself, "I can sell it at the market place for a lot of money!" (1)

Continuing on her way, she thought about what she should do with the money she would get from selling the milk and after a few second she proclaimed, "I shall buy eggs!" (2)

"And what shall I do with the eggs?" She thought for a moment and said, "I shall hatch them and raise chicken. And what shall I do with these chicken?"

"I will sell them in the market. And then what shall I do with the money?" she asked herself all over again, thinking about all the possible things that she could buy if she had a lot of money. (3)

"I will buy a gorgeous dress, of course," she said, laughing aloud and thoroughly enjoying her daydream. "I will then go to a party with this dress and all the handsome, young men will say, 'You're the most beautiful lady in the room. Will you marry me?' And I will toss my head and say, 'Certainly not!' "(4)

Saying these words, the farmer's daughter tossed her head about in the air. Down went the bucket of milk crashing to the ground, and with that, the imaginary eggs, chicken, her dream gown, and the group of adoring young men all disappeared. (5)

Moral of the story: Do not count your chicken before they have hatched. (6)

2 How much did you read? Check [✓] the number that corresponds most closely with where you stopped.

(1) ——— 87 words   (2) ——— 119 words   (3) ——— 188 words

(4) ——— 245 words   (5) ——— 287 words   (6) ——— 300 words

3 Re-read the story, starting from the beginning. Stop reading after one minute. Check [✓] the number that corresponds most closely with where you stopped this time.

(1) ——— 87 words   (2) ——— 119 words   (3) ——— 188 words

(4) ——— 245 words   (5) ——— 287 words   (6) ——— 300 words

Feedback

Repeated readings will increase your reading speed because you know what the text is about. A fluent reader, who is able to comprehend the text, can read at least 250 words in a minute.

The Making of a Millionaire

Before Reading

1 What qualities are most important to have if you want to become a millionaire? Rank the following qualities:

✓✓ = very important, ✓= important, ×= not important. Tell a partner about your ideas.

a. _____ competitiveness   **b.** _____ intelligence   **c.** _____ determination   **d.** _____ kindness
e. _____ confidence   **f.** _____ ambition   **g.** _____ optimism   **h.** _____ frugality

2 Take one minute to skim the text. What is the main idea?

a. _____ The best jobs to have if you want to become a millionaire.
b. _____ Personality traits that most millionaires have in common.

3 Before you start reading, mark down the time.
Starting Time: _____

While Reading

4 Read the article quickly and without stopping. While reading, decide if your answer to question 2 is correct.

After Reading

5 After you finish, mark down the time. Calculate your reading time.
Finishing Time: _____   Reading Time: _____

6 Highlight:
a. the main idea.   **b.** four supporting ideas.

7 Check [✓] the inferences you can make about the text. Underline the statements that help you make the inferences.

a. _____ Lottery winners do not make up the majority of the world's millionaires.
b. _____ Donald Trump made his money from his reality television program.
c. _____ Carlos Slim is a first generation Mexican businessman.
d. _____ Ingvar Kamprad bought Ikea after it became successfully established.
e. _____ Loving what you do is the most important personality trait for millionaires.

8 Re-read the text. Mark your new reading time.
Starting Time: _____   Finishing Time: _____   Reading Time: _____

The Making of a Millionaire

A millionaire is a person with financial assets, not including their home, worth over US$1 million. Today, there are close to 10 million millionaires in the world and while some people have inherited
[5] their wealth, and others have won it, the vast majority of millionaires have worked hard to earn their wealth. Even once they have accumulated a fortune, most only feel comfortable when they are doing something, rather than sitting idle.

[10] Yet if working hard was the only thing needed to make a million dollars, there would be many more millionaires in the world. The many people who work hard but are still not millionaires may be missing certain personality traits that self-made
[15] millionaires tend to have in common, traits such as optimism, a sense of confidence, decisiveness, foresight, frugality, and perhaps most importantly, a love of their job.

Most millionaires are optimists, an important
[20] factor when they encounter a setback or make a mistake. Instead of beating themselves up for it, they use any difficulty as a learning opportunity. Consider Donald Trump, one of the richest real estate developers in the world. In the 1990s,
[25] Trump had financed a number of expensive building projects, but when the U.S. economy suffered, his once prosperous business went $3.5 billion in debt and his own personal finances were $900 million in the red. Instead of giving up,
[30] Trump slowly climbed out of the hole, diversified his interests, including starting a successful reality television show, and he is now a billionaire. As Trump once said, "My policy is to learn from the past, focus on the present, and dream about
[35] the future. I'm a firm believer in learning from adversity. Often the worst of times can turn to your advantage – my life is a study of that."

Another pair of characteristics that many millionaires share is decisiveness and foresight
[40] – they act immediately when a good opportunity arises and they always seem to have a plan driving their actions. The Mexican businessman Carlos Slim, one of the richest men in the world, is an embodiment of that. Slim is an astute judge
[45] of the markets and understands the importance of acting quickly. When the Mexican government was selling off Telemex, the state telephone company, in the 1990s, Slim was especially interested in the little-used cellular service as
[50] he had an idea for building its customer base by selling prepaid phones. Other executives had resisted the plan, but they were silenced when they saw Slim's results. The new business filled an enormous need, and the customer base grew
[55] by 66 percent every year for 15 years. Slim clearly recognized the needs of his customers and responded to them before anyone else.

Even though millionaires are wealthy enough to buy whatever they might want, most focus
[60] on accumulating, rather than spending, their wealth. Many millionaires are frugal when it comes to spending money on themselves. Ingvar Kamprad, the founder and owner of IKEA, the Swedish international furniture chain, is a well–
[65] documented example of this. Kamprad drives a 15-year-old Volvo, flies only economy class, and encourages all his employees to always write on both sides of a piece of paper in order to cut down on costs and waste. There must be something to
[70] his spendthrift ways as he is a billionaire.

Finally, the one characteristic most frequently considered vital in becoming a millionaire is being passionate about what you do. It is much easier to spend hours each day working at something you
[75] believe in, find interesting, and derive satisfaction from. As Steve Jobs, the billionaire founder of Apple computers has said, "Your work is going to fill a large part of your life, and the only way to be truly satisfied is to do what you believe is great
[80] work, and the only way to do great work is to love what you do."

Word Work

9 Match the word chunk with its definition.

a. have in common   •   •   **i.** do nothing

b. beat (yourself) up for (something)   •   •   **ii.** become financially stable again

c. in the red   •   •   **iii.** share

d. climb out of the hole   •   •   **iv.** in debt

e. sit idle   •   •   **v.** feel bad about something you did

10 Choose three chunks and make sentences about yourself or a friend.

a. _____

b. _____

c. _____

Money-making Whiz Kid Unfairly Targeted

Before Reading

1 Tell a partner anything you know about buying and selling stocks or other investments.

2 Quickly scan the text and highlight names, dates, and numbers. Answer the following questions.
   a. What is the SEC?
   b. How old was Jonathan when he became interested in the stock market?
   c. In which years did Jonathan make the bulk of his money?
   d. How much did Jonathan have to pay back to the SEC?

3 Before you start reading, mark down the time.
Starting Time: _____

While Reading

4 Decide what you think of Jonathan.

After Reading

5 After you finish, mark down the time. Calculate your reading time.
Finishing Time: _____   Reading Time: _____

6 What did you think of Jonathan? Check [✓] your answers.

_____ intelligent	_____ strange	_____ hardworking
_____ interesting	_____ funny	_____ normal
_____ frugal	_____ determined	_____ confident
_____ scared	_____ optimistic	_____ friendly

7 Talk about the article with a partner.
a. I think the story is …   **b.** I think Jonathan …
c. I think the SEC was …   **d.** I think Jonathan's parents …
e. I think Jonathan's teachers …

8 Check [✓] the biases shown in the text.
a. _____ headline   **b.** _____ photo   **c.** _____ imbalance   **d.** _____ word choice
e. _____ statistic and numbers

Money-making Whiz Kid Unfairly Targeted

Jonathan Lebed appeared to be an average adolescent; a fairly quiet boy and avid baseball fan who spent most of his free time on his computer. Yet, Jonathan was not playing video games; he
[5] spent his free time making thousands of dollars a day trading stocks on the Internet from his bedroom. By the time Jonathan was fifteen, he had already made over $800,000.

Jonathan's fascination with the stock market
[10] began when he was 11 and would monitor the prices of stocks owned by his father. By 12 he was hooked on the market and he convinced his parents to allow him to invest $8,000 in AOL stock. Although his father was initially against it,
[15] he realized his son knew something about the markets when the price of AOL shares rose and his son made a tidy profit. Jonathan and a few friends entered a nationwide stock-picking competition for students. His team was consistently placed in
[20] the top three, until the last month when some of their stocks crashed and they ended up in fourth place. However, it was enough of an education to convince Jonathan and his parents that he had a talent for picking stocks. He had realized that with
[25] careful research and thoughtful analysis, anybody could be an amateur stock market analyst.

Jonathan then started his own website designed to promote penny stocks, stocks that could be bought for a few cents and might eventually sell
[30] for a couple of dollars. His website promoted the stocks of companies that Jonathan found interesting as well as those that people he had met on the Internet thought had potential. At its peak, the site had about 1,500 visitors a day, not
[35] bad for a kid who was still going to school full-time. But then his parents got a call from one of the U.S. financial authorities, the Securities and Exchange Commission (SEC).

Jonathan had posted stock advice from a man
[40] that the SEC was investigating for fraud and they believed that Jonathan had accepted money from the man as payment for posting the fraudulent information. But Jonathan had done nothing illegal and after eight hours of interrogation, he
[45] was allowed to go back home where he went right back to doing what he did best, Internet trading.

Many teenagers look for a way to escape the tedium of adolescent life and Jonathan was no different. He lived in a suburban neighborhood
[50] with not much to do, especially for someone without a driver's license. The Internet provided the perfect place for Jonathan to appear to be an adult. His online persona was mature, made sophisticated stock picks, and people respected
[55] his choices because they usually made money for them. Adults did not treat him like a 14-year-old kid because they did not know his age and they believed he was an educated and experienced trader.

[60] In order to juggle his daily school responsibilities and his Internet trading life, Jonathan would rise early in the morning, buy some stocks and then from 5 a.m. – 8 a.m., post about 200 messages on financial chat sites promoting those companies.
[65] During his fifth period, when he was allowed to study in the library, Jonathan would use one of the school computers to continue to promote his stock choices. Other students knew what he was doing and often followed his advice when they
[70] realized that his picks often paid off.
When he would get home, Jonathan would spend

the afternoon and evening promoting his stocks before selling them at the height of their value. From September of 1999 to February 2000, [75] Jonathan was making thousands of dollars a day. His lowest daily take was $12,000 and his highest was $74,000.

Jonathan and his friends thought he was a stock market whiz kid, beating stock traders at their [80] own game, but the SEC thought otherwise.

Once again, the SEC called Jonathan in for questioning. This time they accused him of manipulating the stock markets and threatened to prosecute him unless he paid back all of his [85] earnings. It was the first time that a minor had been charged with securities fraud. According to the SEC, he was guilty of "pumping and dumping" i.e. buying stocks, then lying or at least misleading others about their earning potential which would [90] artificially raise their price before profiting off the false information by selling the stocks. The SEC and Jonathan eventually settled the matter out of court, with Jonathan reportedly paying $285,000 but keeping the rest of the money he had made [95] from his stock trades, estimated to be close to half a million dollars.

Although the SEC publicly made a case against Jonathan, as a warning to other Internet traders who might be doing similar dealings, it has not [100] deterred him or his followers. When Jonathan graduated from high school he started his own stock promotion website and an investor relations firm. Now he just promotes the stock and leaves the buying to others though.

Word Work

9 **Correct the highlighted word chunks.**

a. Jonathan made **a neat profit** off his Internet stock investments.
_____

b. Investors are always upset when their **stocks collide**.
_____

c. Investors usually try to sell off their stocks when prices are **at their summit.**
_____

d. I am going to check out Jonathan's new website and maybe I will **chase his advice** and buy some stock.
_____

e. Jonathan was such a **fast kid** at making money on the stock exchange, even his teachers asked him for stock tips.
_____

10 **Choose three chunks and make sentences about yourself or a friend.**

a. _____
b. _____
c. _____

5 Advertising

Warm Up

1 Decide the product each picture could be used to promote.

a. _____ b. _____ c. _____ d. _____

2 Tell a partner which one you like best.

3 Check [✓] the statements you agree with. Discuss your answers with a partner.

a. _____ Each picture features one or more beautiful women.
b. _____ Each picture gives you information about the product it is promoting.
c. _____ Each picture shows the women using the product they are promoting.
d. _____ Each picture is effective.
e. _____ Each picture is memorable.

Reading Strategy: Synthesizing information

A reader will usually **synthesize information** while reading and also after reading a text.
Synthesizing is bringing together information from different parts of a text or from different texts to create new ideas.

When you synthesize information you can:
• compare and contrast information from one or more texts.
• reduce and summarize ideas from different parts of the text.
• make connections with previous knowledge and experience.

Synthesizing information helps readers decide what is important and what is irrelevant in a text. It also helps the reader form opinions, make judgments, and draw conclusions about the subject or topic of the text.

Strategy in Focus

1 Read the texts. Note the ideas from the texts in the chart. Complete the chart with other information or ideas from your own knowledge and experience of advertising.

Information in both texts	Information only in text i	Information only in text ii	Other information

i. Memorable Advertising

Oliviero Toscani believes that advertising should be more than just about selling products. Toscani, a fashion photographer and former creative director of Benetton, has spent years generating controversy with his advertising promotions that have focused more on artistic or unusual images than on the products being promoted. Past campaigns have included a graphic image of a baby taken a few minutes after it was born; three human hearts labeled white, black and yellow; a priest kissing a nun; and a person dying from AIDS. In all of those campaigns, the company's clothing was absent and the only clue to the advertiser's brand was Benetton's logo discretely printed.

Toscani's campaign for another Italian clothing company featured a nude photograph of a famous French actress who has struggled for years with an eating disorder. The photograph of the dangerously thin actress next to the words, 'No Anorexia', was plastered on billboards during Milan's fashion week. Like his other campaigns, this one received mixed reviews, with some applauding his attempt to raise awareness of eating disorders and others complaining that he was trivializing a serious health problem for profit. For Toscani, who thinks that the purpose of advertising is to improve the world, such criticism is unlikely to stop his artistic vision.

ii. Conscientious Advertising

Most companies use advertising to promote their brand, sell their products and increase revenues. They are less concerned about the global influence their advertisements could have on highlighting social issues. In this regards, Benetton stands out.

After a period of successful but controversial campaigns, the Italian clothing company decided to focus on raising awareness of global concerns. The company has focused advertising campaigns on issues such as ending hunger, fighting poverty, promoting development in Africa, and encouraging volunteering. In 2001, they collaborated with the United Nations Volunteers to showcase the impact that volunteering has on the world. In 2003, they teamed up with another UN agency, the World Food Program to emphasize hunger as the world's most pressing problem. In 2008, equitable and sustainable development in Africa became the centerpiece of their advertisement campaigns. It highlights the importance of how African people can fight poverty, promote development, and create a sustainable future through their work as fishermen, farmers, and tailors.

Feedback

You will have your own answers depending on what you think are the important ideas and your life experience. Both texts talk about Benetton advertisements and how they do not show the product; you may conclude that this is unusual based on your experience of seeing other advertisements.

Before Reading

1 Skim the text. Look at the title and the picture then read the first and last sentence of each paragraph. What is the main idea of the text?

a. George Clooney is a good example of how using a celebrity in advertising is effective.
b. Advertisements use celebrities because many people think copying celebrities leads to a better life.
c. People who buy the products advertised by celebrities, such as clothes and cigarettes, have a lot of fun.

2 Before you start reading, mark down the time.

Starting Time: _____

While Reading

3 Read the article quickly and without stopping. While reading, decide if your answer to question 1 is correct.

After Reading

4 After you finish, mark down the time. Calculate your reading time.

Finishing Time: _____   Reading Time: _____

5 Ask a partner the following questions about the text.

a. Which ideas do you agree with?   b. Which ideas do you disagree with?

6 Review the warm up texts. Complete the chart.

Information in the Warm Up texts and Reading 1	Information only in Reading 1	Other information

Who do You Want to Be?
Imitation in Advertising

For years businesses have used different psychological strategies in **their** advertising to sell products and services. Understanding the psychological factors that motivate people to
[5] buy something can help a business sell more of their goods. Businesses use advertising to send a message saying that their product will do more than provide something practical or useful. The message is that the product can help **you** be a
[10] better person or lead a better life as well.

One common strategy used in advertising is to appeal to people's need to imitate or copy someone **they** admire. This type of advertisement shows a celebrity using a product with the hope
[15] that viewers want to look like the celebrity, have the celebrity's lifestyle, or have the celebrity's power and influence, and that purchasing the product will help the buyer achieve these things. For example, the actor George Clooney has been
[20] paid to advertise amongst other things, a car in Japan, clothes in Italy, and coffee in a number of countries. He does not need to be an expert driver, be a fashion designer, or know anything about coffee to make these advertisements
[25] successful.

Some people may be encouraged to feel they will also gain greater self-esteem from imitating the appearance of celebrities or people they think are superior. Some young people may copy the
[30] clothing styles of popular actors or musicians because they think friends, colleagues, and even strangers will see them as being similar to the person advertising the products. On some subconscious level, the buyer is made to believe

[35] that by wearing a watch brand that Tiger Woods advertises, he or she will feel as successful and admired as Tiger Woods.

Advertisers have noticed that people are more likely to buy products advertised by people
[40] who are shown as being rich and having fun. An advertiser might show actors having fun in an advert because their target audience will then think they can achieve the same financial success and have a more enjoyable life. They
[45] hope people will buy the product or service because it is associated in the advertisement with a successful and fun lifestyle.

Where they are permitted, advertisements for cigarettes often rely on appealing to an
[50] association with fun and pleasure. The advertisers focus the consumers' attention on the fun that the characters are seen to be experiencing in their advertisement in order to draw attention away from the inherent risks of cigarette smoking.
[55] Many people do not notice that there are often no cigarettes in many cigarette advertisements. These advertisements are aimed at existing smokers and try to influence the consumer to identify their particular brand of cigarettes with the
[60] people having fun. This is called 'peripheral route advertising' whereas 'central route advertising' places the emphasis on the product by stating facts about the product and highlighting the use of the product in the advertisement.

[65] The main thing about relying on imitation (or aspiration) as an advertising strategy is that the consumer must see some advantage in imitating the person in the advertisement. No one will copy behavior just for the sake of it. They do it
[70] for greed, enjoyment, self-esteem, or some other benefit. For imitation to work it must be connected to some stronger appeal. One interesting aspect of imitation is that its effectiveness decreases with the age of the target audience. Advertisements
[75] that rely on imitation are most effective when aimed at teens and preteens and are less effective with young adults.

7 | **Find these words in the text. Decide what they refer to.**

a. their (line 2):
   i. businesses   ii. psychological strategies   iii. products and services

b. you (line 9):
   i. advertisers   ii. people reading this text   iii. people who see the advertisement

c. they (line 13):
   i. people   ii. businesses   iii. products

Word Work

8 | **Circle the correct word chunk for each sentence.**

a. The coach dropped Pablo from the soccer team to **send a message / say a message** to all the players that they have to attend all the training sessions.

b. I told Aya it was my birthday with **a hope which / the hope that** she would organize a surprise party.

c. School kids who are not good at academic subjects often **win self-esteem / gain self-esteem** from sport, music or art.

d. Donald Trump **achieved financial success / won financial victory** in the real estate business.

e. Using beautiful women in advertisements can be an effective way to sell products to a **target people / target audience** of young men.

9 | **Choose three chunks and make sentences about yourself or a friend.**

a. _____

b. _____

c. _____

Before Reading

1 Check [✓] the statements that are true about synthesizing information.
a. _____ Synthesizing means taking information from different sources to make new ideas.
b. _____ You combine information from previous texts, previous knowledge and life experience to the information in the new text.
c. _____ You should not create your own ideas when reading a text.
d. _____ You can take ideas from different parts of the text to help you summarize.
e. _____ You should only think about the ideas presented in the text you are reading.
f. _____ You can combine the ideas in the text with your own knowledge to make own judgments and draw your own conclusions.

2 Take two minutes to skim the text. What is the main idea?

While Reading

3 Circle the images you visualize while reading the text.

TV commercial for a cleaning product	a car commercial	a woman at home	a celebrity
a product you have bought	your family	an old commercial	attractive people

After Reading

4 Tell a partner about the images visualized.

5 What is the main idea in these paragraphs?
Paragraph 2
a. Gender stereotyping has improved since the 1970s.
b. Men and women are still presented in commercials in traditional roles.
Paragraph 4
a. The idea that happiness and beauty is connected to being slim and athletic is the same for men and women.
b. Slim, athletic, and handsome men attract more beautiful women than overweight men.
Paragraph 5
a. Commercials for boys are more effective if they include a lot of action.
b. Gender stereotyping can be seen most clearly and is used more often in commercials aimed at children.

6 Check the judgments you made and conclusions you drew.
a. _____ TV commercials would be more successful if they presented women in more powerful roles.
b. _____ TV commercials are very effective and do not need to change.
c. _____ TV commercials in my country are offensive to both men and women.

Stereotyping in Advertising

BEFORE   AFTER

[1] Gender stereotypes are more obvious in TV commercials than in regular TV programming even though men and women appear equally often as central characters in commercials.

[2] Since the early 1970s, gender stereotyping in the USA has decreased somewhat, but women are still most often presented in the home in the role of wife and / or mother. When they are depicted as employed, their range of occupations is broader than it once was, but it is still traditionally "feminine". Women are most often seen in ads for food and they are more likely than men to be shown using the products they advertise, for example cooking, cleaning, and talking on a phone. Men, whose depiction as husband and / or father has increased, are still more frequently presented in other roles, especially ones in the business world. Men are also more likely to advertise automotive products and alcohol.

[3] Women in commercials are much younger than the men and relations between the sexes are typically portrayed in very traditional ways. For example, detergent commercials still primarily depict a woman worrying about getting the dirt off her husband's clothes rather than vice versa. And it is often more important for women to be attractive. On the other hand, men are increasingly likely to be the butt of jokes, especially when they show ignorance about nutrition and child care. The most striking difference between women and men in commercials is the fact that men predominate (83-90 percent) in voice-overs, even when the products are aimed at women. Thus again, the voice of authority is male, even though research suggests that female voice-overs are just as effective.

[4] On children's shows, stereotypes in commercials are everywhere especially those focused on gender roles. Boys appear more often than girls and they have more positive roles. Boys are more likely to be portrayed in active roles, girls in passive ones. Indeed, commercials aimed at boys have a different format than commercials aimed at girls. Commercials aimed at boys have rapid action, frequent cuts, loud music and sound effects, and frequent scene changes. In contrast, commercials aimed at girls contain much softer changes from one scene to the next scene, calmer background music, and female narration. Children as young as six recognize these distinctions, which means that even if the content of a commercial does not say the product is for boys or girls, the style in which it is produced might. But most often the content specifies the gender of the product as well. Toys are clearly gender-labeled, with action toys aimed at boys and domestic and cosmetic toys tagged for girls. Racial stereotyping is also often prevalent in children's commercials, with children from ethnic minorities almost always in supporting roles or not used at all.

[5] One thing that is the same for men and women in television commercials is the actors' body type and what this is supposed to mean for your happiness. Regardless of the job or function of a character on television commercials, the vast majority of the men and women are slim and athletic looking; the men are handsome and the women pretty. The media portrays these body types as attractive, desirable, and "good". Conversely, bodies that do not meet this almost impossible goal frequently are, consciously or unconsciously, regarded as "bad", undesirable, or ugly. Consider an extremely popular advertisement for a national fast food sandwich chain in the USA. Jared, the main character of the television commercials, claims to have lost a lot of weight, while on a diet consisting solely of the restaurant's sandwiches. Jared's "before"

pictures show him much larger than his current size, but they also show him alone, with no friends or family. In contrast, however, his "after" photos show him not only thinner, but also constantly in the presence of a beautiful woman, presumably his partner. The advertising message is clear; fat means you will be ugly, unhappy, and alone, while thin means happy, popular, and have an attractive partner. Through these commercials, Jared assumed celebrity status, solely on the basis that his body has changed to approximate more closely the current idea of attractiveness created by television.

[6] Despite the huge changes in men and women's roles in the USA over the last few decades, stereotypes in TV remain, especially in TV advertising.

Adopted from Basow. Gender: Stereotypes and Roles, 3E. © 1992 Wadsworth, a part of Cengage Learning, Inc. Reproduced by permission. www.cengage.com/permissions.

Word Work

7 **Complete the sentences with a word chunk from the text. Change the verb tense where necessary.**

the butt of jokes	central characters	research suggests	television commercials
child care	in the business world	body type	the vast majority

a. Although a few students in the class did not pass the test, _____ studied hard, got good grades, and learned a lot of English.

b. I love watching the TV series Lost. Jack and Kate are the _____. They are always in trouble or in the middle of the action.

c. One of the most expensive things about having a baby in New York is paying for _____ when you go back to work.

d. I started working out and went on a diet because I wanted to change my _____ and feel healthier.

e. It is much more common to find women in positions of authority in the teaching and caring professions than _____.

f. I have read a lot of articles and papers about learning English and the _____ if you increase the amount you read, you will not only improve your reading skills but also your speaking and writing.

g. When I was a child I was always _____ for the other children because I could not speak properly.

h. Jodi Foster was in a number of _____ as a child before she became a famous movie actor.

8 **Choose three chunks and make sentences about yourself or a friend.**
  a. _____
  b. _____
  c. _____

Reflection

▶ Which was your favorite text in this unit? Why?

▶ Which reading strategies did you use in this unit?

▶ Which new word chunks will you make an effort to use in the next five days? Choose at least five.

6

The Art of Color

Warm Up

1 Which colors would you expect to find in each painting? List the colors underneath each picture.

_____   _____   _____
_____   _____   _____
_____   _____   _____
_____   _____   _____
_____   _____   _____

2 How do different colors affect the way you feel?

Reading Strategy: Summarizing

While and after reading a text, it is often useful to **summarize** what you have read. You can do this in your mind, and you can also write a **summary**.

When you **summarize** a text, you identify the main ideas and other important details. It is not necessary to remember everything that you have read.

These questions will help you **summarize** a text:

- What is the text about?
- Who is the text about?
- What happens? When? Where?
- Why did the author write the text?

It is important to give credit to the author who wrote the original text. The author's name and the title of the article is usually mentioned near the beginning of a written summary. Because the point of a summary is usually to re-tell the author's main idea and most important details, you should not include your personal opinion about whether you liked or disliked the article in your summary.

Strategy in Focus

1 **As you read, think about the following questions.**

   a. What is the text about?

   b. What are the most important details?

   c. Why did the author write the text?

Are You Wearing the Right Color?

Many people are not aware that the color of their clothing can either make them look fresh and radiant or tired and worn out. By analyzing your skin tone, eye color and hair color, you can determine which "season" you are and this will help you choose the best colors for your wardrobe.

People who are "winters" usually have pale white, yellowish-olive, or dark skin colors. Their hair color is generally brown and they have dark colored eyes. Beyonce and Zhang Ziyi are famous winters. Winters look great in rich, intense colors like red, navy blue, black, bright white, and hot pink. Colors that will make them look unhealthy and tired include earthy tones and more subdued colors like orange, gold, and beige.

"Summers" often have pale, pink skin and are often natural blondes or brunettes with light colored eyes. Reese Witherspoon and Jennifer Aniston are both well-known examples of summers. Summers should choose soft neutral colors, pastels, and other muted colors like powder blue, dusty pink, lavender, and pale yellow. Unlike winters, summers should avoid intense colors because they will make them look worn out. Like winters, they should also avoid earth tones and orange.

Those who have an "autumn" complexion usually have red or brown hair and light brown eyes. Julia Roberts and Angelina Jolie fall into this category. They can wear rich or muted warm colors that are seen in autumn leaves and spices, such as olive, orange, gold, dark brown, and warm gray. However, they should definitely avoid bright colors, pastels, or black and white as all of these will make them look pale, tired and faded.

The final season is "spring" and these people usually have light ivory colored skin. Hair coloring can be golden blonde, auburn, or strawberry blond and eye color is either light blue or green. Freckles and rosy cheeks are other characteristics of this season. Nicole Kidman and Cameron Diaz are true springs and look best in pale, soft colors like peach, golden yellow and brown, ivory, bright greens, true reds, and aquamarine. Springs should avoid wearing black and white, pastels, and certain blues like navy.

Feedback

a. The text describes how people can determine which season they are and which colors they should and should not wear. b. The most important details are that a person is characterized as either being a winter, summer, autumn, or spring depending on their skin tone, eye color and natural hair color. c. The author wrote the text to help people determine their season so they would know which colors will help them look their best.

Before Reading

1 Based on your own opinion, which color (red, blue, or green) do you associate with the following words? Write your answer next to the word.

a. _____ life   **b.** _____ energetic   **c.** _____ calming
d. _____ ocean   **e.** _____ good fortune   **f.** _____ anger
g. _____ sadness   **h.** _____ war

2 Before you start reading, mark down your starting time.
Starting Time: _____

While Reading

3 As you read, think about the following questions and highlight the answers in the text.
a. What is the text about?
b. What are the most important details of the text?

After Reading

4 After you finish, mark down the time. Calculate your reading time.
Finishing Time: _____   Reading Time: _____

5 Associate the text with your personal experiences. Tell a partner:
a. about your favorite color and why it is your favorite.
b. one interesting fact that you already knew about color and one that you learned.
c. if a certain color has ever had a physical effect on you.

6 Which of these choices best sums up what the story is about?
a. The cultural reasons why pink is Anna's favorite color.
b. The physical effects that certain colors have upon people.
c. The different meanings and reactions that people have to certain colors.

7 Choose three sentences that best complete a summary of the texts.
a. Color may symbolize different values or ideas depending on cultural background.
b. Green is symbolic of eternal life in Japan.
c. Color may also cause physical reactions in people.
d. However, some people's favorite color might just be a personal choice.
e. The color red can stimulate someone's appetite and is a good color to have in restaurants.

Color Symbolism

Three-year-old Anna loves anything pink – her favorite clothes, dolls, and toys are all varying shades of the color. Many little girls like Anna will choose pink when asked their favorite color,
[5] but why? And why is pink often a color for girls and blue a color for boys? The answer depends mainly on personal experiences and cultural values because colors mean different things to different people around the world.

[10] The meaning of a certain color may change depending on your cultural background. Green is one of these colors. To the Egyptians, green was a sacred color and represented the hope and joy of spring. Green is also an important
[15] color to Muslims and along with blue it represents paradise. Meanwhile in Japan, it is said to symbolize eternal life.

It is said that green is the most restful color for the human eye and that it has great healing
[20] power, having the ability to soothe pain, alleviate depression, and relax people both mentally and physically. In fact, people who work in green environments have been found to have fewer stomach aches, while a green environment is
[25] beneficial for teething infants, and believe it or not, when London's Blackfriars Bridge was painted green the number of people committing suicide there dropped by 34 percent.

For many people, red is a favorite color. The color
[30] of fire and blood, red has been seen as symbolic of passion, love, energy, and war. In many cultures, red is associated with prosperity and good luck. In Hindu, Islamic, and Chinese cultures red is a traditional color that brides wear. In China, it
[35] is also an important color associated with the Lunar New Year. Many Chinese households are decorated with red and children are often given money in a red envelope to bring good fortune in the New Year.

[40] Many people believe that red can increase energy and enthusiasm. The color can cause a person's blood pressure, heartbeat, and pulse rate to rise. In addition, many restaurant decorators believe that red causes people to feel hungry
[45] and will include accents of red in the restaurant to stimulate customers' appetites. Red is also a color that easily catches a person's eye and is often used in advertising to get people to act quickly. Many commercial websites will have a
[50] red "Buy Now" button to encourage people to make a purchase.

Blue, like green and red, is another universal color and is associated with the water and the sky. For many it is symbolic of protection, faith, and
[55] religious beliefs. In Greece, blue is considered to offer protection against evil. People who believe this often wear a blue necklace or bracelet. However in Iran, blue symbolizes faith and paradise and is used as a color in many mosaics
[60] in the country's mosques.

Blue is another calming color and it has been found that people sleep better in blue rooms. Unlike red, blue suppresses appetite and slows metabolism so restaurants would be wise to avoid
[65] too much blue in their decor. However, if you are thinking about losing weight, some people suggest that blue plates can help as we seem to eat less when eating from them.

The next time you are deciding on what to wear
[70] or what color to decorate your room, think about the color carefully. Not only may your color choice mean something different in different cultures, but it may also produce a physical reaction in you or someone nearby.

Word Work

8 Correct the mistakes in these word chunks.

a. The meaning of color may change depending on your **cultural environment.**

_____

b. **It is told** that green is the most restful color for the human eye.

_____

c. It also has great healing power and it can **soothe hurting.**

_____

d. The color can cause a person's blood pressure, heartbeat and **pulse beat** to rise.

_____

e. Unlike red, blue **holds up appetite** and slows metabolism.

_____

9 Choose three chunks and make sentences about yourself or a friend.

a. _____

b. _____

c. _____

Before Reading

1 Skim the text. What is the main idea?
   a. The academic training of the pop artist, Takashi Murakami.
   b. The popularity and commercialization of Takashi Murakami's artwork.
   c. The work and life of the pop artist, Takashi Murakami.

While Reading

2 Read the text more carefully and check your hypothesis.

After Reading

3 Decide if you agree [✓] or disagree [×] with these judgments.
   a. _____ Takashi Murakami's art sounds interesting.
   b. _____ Takashi Murakami's ideas and art are strange.
   c. _____ Takashi Murakami seems more concerned with making a lot of money than making quality art.

4 Decide if the bold statements in the text are fact (F) or opinion (O) according to the text.
   a. _____   b. _____   c. _____   d. _____   e. _____

5 Check [✓] the inferences that you can make.
   a. _____ Takashi Murakami's art has featured on backpacks and purses.
   b. _____ Andy Warhol's art was very expensive.
   c. _____ Murakami has more than one art factory where he produces his work.
   d. _____ Murakami believes that museums are more popular than movie theaters.
   e. _____ Murakami was good at academics as well as creating art.
   f. _____ Murakami is more interested in making money than serious art.

6 Choose the best ending to the summary.
   In the article, *The Colorful Mind of Takashi Murakami*, the author introduces us to the contemporary Japanese pop artist.
   a. The text compares Murakami to Warhol and focuses on how the two are similar, yet different. Both artists had assistants who helped them create their art, but Murakami's can be bought by more people.
   b. The text briefly describes Murakami's academic training but focuses more on how his art has been produced and commercialized. Although Murakami has a very successful business producing commercial art, he is also concerned with producing fine art.
   c. The text details the commercial success of Takashi Murakami. For instance, he partnered with Louis Vuitton and helped with a design that sold over 300 million dollars-worth of products.

The Colorful Mind of Takashi Murakami

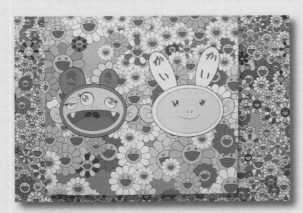

When you first see a Murakami creation, you might feel like you have stumbled across the marriage of Disney's *Alice in Wonderland* and Japanese animation. Cute, candy-colored cartoon
[5] characters with large eyes and exaggerated body parts feature predominantly in his paintings. Other images like blinking eyes, smiling flowers, and colorful mushrooms float across his work. (a) **It is a psychedelic, dream-like world of immense**
[10] **creativity.**

Takashi Murakami is often compared to the iconic American pop artist Andy Warhol. Like Warhol, Murakami employs assistants to help produce his colorful art, and his work is inspired by everyday
[15] consumer culture. (b) **Murakami's work can be enjoyed by everyone.** Not only can it be seen on the walls of well-known art museums and galleries, but it can also be found on clothing and in fashion. His work has even hit supermarket
[20] aisles with kids able to buy bubble gum-filled plastic figurines designed by him that cost just a few dollars.

Many artists shun this type of commercialization but for Murakami, art is more about "creating
[25] goods and selling them than about exhibitions." As he once said, (c) **"Few people come to museums;** much bigger are movie theaters." adding that museums are for old-style media. And to the average bystander, Murakami would seem more
[30] like a savvy businessman than one of today's most influential pop artists. He cites Bill Gates' tips on business efficiency as influential in the management of Hiropon, one of his art factories outside of Tokyo. (d) **The factory employs**
[35] **accountants, publicists, and managers in addition to the twenty-five assistants who work with Murakami in the creation of his pieces.**

Although interested in business management,
[40] Murakami's main passion has always been art. Growing up in Tokyo in the 1960s and 70s, Murakami was influenced by Japanese popular culture, but was also exposed to American influences in imported movies and music. (e) **He**
[45] **was fascinated by animation and enrolled in the Tokyo National University of Fine Arts and Music where he studied *nihonga*, a Japanese style of painting that combines both Eastern and Western painting techniques.** While at the
[50] university, Murakami saw the exploding popularity of *anime* (Japanese animation) and *manga* (Japanese comics), and he felt that they were much more relevant to contemporary Japanese culture than *nihonga*. Although Murakami would earn his PhD
[55] in *nihonga*, he would make his mark by including *anime* and *manga* influences in his art.

The infusion of pop culture in Murakami's paintings and sculptures is easy to spot. One of his best-known characters is Mr. DOB, a mouse-like
[60] creature with a round head and large, circular ears. Mr. DOB represents a quality that the Japanese call kawaii or "being cute" which embodies many of the images coming from Japanese culture such as Hello Kitty®. He believes these images
[65] provide relief for a stressed society.

In 2003, Murakami gained widespread fame when he partnered with designer Marc Jacobs in a new design for a range of Louis Vuitton purses. The creations featured some of his cartoon
[70] images and bright colors interspersed between the traditional LV logo. Sales of these bags exceeded $300 million and Murakami's style became recognized worldwide.

Despite welcoming this commercial success, [75] Murakami realized that he needed to strengthen his reputation as a "serious" artist. As he once said in an interview, "I need to rebuild the wall between the commercial art and the fine art I do. I need to focus on the fine art side of me for a while." [80] Since then, Murakami has worked hard to achieve that balance and is now recognized as a leading contemporary Japanese artist.

Word Work

7 Rewrite the sentences using the word chunks below. Change the tense when necessary.

widespread fame	average bystander	exploding popularity
make his mark	easy to spot	

a. Takashi Murakami **became very famous** when he partnered with Marc Jacobs to produce a design for Louis Vuitton.

b. The **instant fame** of the Louis Vuitton design surprised everyone, especially Murakami.

c. Murakami's paintings are **quite recognizable** because they are colorful and filled with anime-type images.

d. Takashi Murakami usually dresses in a very relaxed manner and an **ordinary person** might not recognize him on the street.

e. Now that Murakami has achieved **worldwide recognition**, he is busy organizing art exhibits in major cities around the world.

8 Choose three chunks and make sentences about yourself or a friend.
a. _____
b. _____
c. _____

Reflection

▶ Which was your favorite text in this unit? Why?

▶ Which reading strategies did you use in this unit?

▶ Which new word chunks will you make an effort to use in the next five days? Choose at least five.

Review Reading Strategies

- Unit 4: Reading fluency
- Unit 5: Synthesizing information
- Unit 6: Summarizing

1 Which of the above reading strategies do these sentences describe? Read each statement and check [✓] the best answer.

	Reading Fluency	Synthesizing Information	Summarizing
a. Identify the main ideas and other important details.			
b. Compare and contrast information from one or more texts.			
c. The ability to read a text without stopping			
d. Make connections with previous knowledge and experience			
e. Using previewing strategies such as hypothesizing, skimming, and scanning will help you improve this strategy.			

2 Skim the text. What is the main idea?

- a. Most people know only of the culinary benefits of algae.
- b. Scientists have been studying how to use algae as a source of alternative energy for decades.
- c. Companies and governments are researching the potential use of algae as a source of renewable energy.

3 Before you start reading, mark down the time. Read the article quickly and without stopping. After you finish, mark down the time. Calculate your reading time.

Starting Time: _____   Finishing Time: _____   Reading Time: _____

4 Which of these choices best sums up what the text is about?

- a. The potential benefits and problems of using algae as an alternative fuel.
- b. The reasons why Valcent will be a leader in the algae industry.
- c. The financial and ecological reasons why algae should be used for biofuels.

5 Check [✓] the judgments you made and conclusions you drew.

- a. _____ Growing and using algae for biofuels is much better than growing corn and soybeans.
- b. _____ Governments are only investigating using algae as a source of fuel because the price of oil is high.
- c. _____ The use of algae as an oil is more important than its use in cooking and as a thickening agent.

The Power and Potential of Algae

[1] Algae have always been an important link in the aquatic food chain for their vital role in being the major source of food for fish. However, their importance to humans is often not widely understood. Perhaps best known for their use in Japanese cooking, algae can also be used as a thickening agent in toothpaste, shaving cream, paint, and ice cream. However, Glen Kertz, a plant physiologist and entrepreneur, is most excited about their recently discovered application as a potential energy source.

[2] Kertz, president and CEO of Valcent Products, is a leader in the research on growing and transforming algae into usable oil. About 50 percent of algae's weight is an oil which can be used to make biodiesel for cars, trucks, and airplanes. Kertz's company has developed a system called Vertigro, which grows algae in a closed, vertical system of long rows of moving plastic bags. This system allows more sunlight to reach the algae, enabling it to photosynthesize faster. And unlike other crops now being used for biodiesel such as corn and soybeans, the growing algae do not take up a lot of space which could otherwise be used to grow agricultural food products. As Kertz explains, using algae he can produce about 100,000 gallons of oil a year per acre (153,000 liters/hectare), compared to corn, which only produces 30 gallons per acre and soybeans which only produce 50 gallons per acre.

[3] Research suggests that algae may also help slow the rate of global warming. Algae processing plants have the potential of using carbon dioxide (CO_2), which is one of the leading contributors to greenhouse gases and global warming. Algae need CO_2 for photosynthesis, so by placing algae "farms" next to coal-fired power stations or other polluting manufacturing plants, algae can also help cut back on the harmful emissions of CO_2 these release into the atmosphere.

[4] The use of algae as an alternative fuel is not a novel idea. Starting back in the late 1970s, the U.S. Department of Energy studied it as a viable option to compete with fossil fuels like petroleum and coal, but at that time, the cost of fossil fuels was extremely low and the research was abandoned. However, with the rapid increase in oil prices and concerns about dwindling oil supplies, interest has surged in exploring this field. Governments and industries are spending time and money on how to best harness the potential of algae with the hope that they will help solve their oil-energy dependence.

[5] One U.S. company claims that it can turn algae into a "green crude" that can be processed by oil refineries into gasoline and diesel for existing vehicles. Furthermore, Jason Pyle, Chief Executive of Sapphire Energy, believes that the refining process of his "green crude" is much cleaner than that of existing crude oil. The company reports it can already produce versions of jet fuel, diesel, and gasoline, and Pyle says Sapphire Energy expects to reach full commercial scale in five years and hopes to be making a tidy profit at some point in the near future.

[6] Airlines like Continental, Virgin, Air New Zealand, and KLM are already partnering with the business world and universities to test out biofuels. It is said that both Air New Zealand and KLM are piloting test flights using kerosene fuel made from algae, and they believe they will be able to reduce costs and carbon dioxide emission by using this new product.

[7] Although algae farming does not cause deforestation or take up valuable food growing space, many are still skeptical about its efficacy as a fuel source. Some are concerned that the combustion process may add harmful nitrogen oxide to the air and others worry that the emissions coming from algae-fueled vehicles will still be as damaging to the atmosphere as fossil fuels. Others are waiting until a large-scale processing system has been developed before they fully invest in the algae biofuel market.

Comprehension Check

1 The word "application" in paragraph 1 is closest in meaning to:
  a. form   **b.** use   **c.** ability   **d.** apply

2 In paragraph 3, the author implies that using algae has a potential:
  a. social benefit   **b.** fuel benefit   **c.** financial benefit   **d.** ecological benefit

3 In paragraph 4, the word "they" refers to:
  a. algae   **b.** energy industries   **c.** governments   **d.** researchers

4 In paragraph 6, the author mentions KLM and Air New Zealand as an example of:
  a. companies that are working with Valcent to test their "green crude".
  b. government-controlled businesses that are testing algae biofuels.
  c. companies that will be testing the efficacy of algae biofuels.
  d. companies that are only concerned with cutting down on their costs

5 Which of the following is NOT a benefit of algae mentioned in the text?
  a. food for marine life   **b.** an important source of vitamins
  c. a thickening agent for ice cream   **d.** a way of reducing greenhouses gases

6 Check [✓] the inferences you can make about the text. Underline the words, phrases, or sentences that support your inferences
  a. _____ Sapphire Energy has not proved that its algae refining process is cleaner than others.
  b. _____ Growing algae for biofuel has less of an impact on the agricultural sector than other biofuel crops.
  c. _____ Everyone should invest in algae because it will replace petroleum as the fuel of the future.
  d. _____ Coal and manufacturing plants produce a lot of CO_2 emissions.

More Word Chunks

1 Use these word chunks to write sentences about the text without looking at page 61.
  a. research suggests : _____
  b. with the hope that: _____
  c. a tidy profit: _____
  d. the business world: _____
  e. it is said: _____

2 Match the word chunk from Units 4, 5, and 6 with its definition. Then choose one word chunk and write a sentence about yourself or someone you know.
  a. a tidy profit   i.   a specific group for which advertising is directed
  b. climb out of the hole   ii. do something that gets you attention
  c. target audience   iii. quite a large amount of money left after expenses
  d. make (your) mark   iv. a person who is present at an event but not participating in it
  e. average bystander   v.   become financially stable again

3 | In Unit 4 we learned about the word chunk "in the red", which means to be in debt.

Because it is a new company, it is **in the red** right now, but it should become profitable in the near future.

Here are some other word chunks involving color with their definitions:

red tape	excess bureaucracy, rules that do not seem necessary and make things happen slowly
a red-eye flight	a flight that leaves late at night and arrives early the next morning
in the black	make a profit, when a person / company makes more money than it spends – opposite of 'in the red'
pitch black	very dark
black out	lose consciousness
blue-collar job	work involving physical labor, often in a factory
blue in the face	do something for a long time without success
white-collar job	work that takes place in an office

Complete the sentences with a word chunk from the box above.

a. I took a _____ that left New York at 7:00 p.m. and arrived in London at 6.00 a.m. the next morning.

b. My English teacher can sometimes explain things until she is _____, but for some reason I still have problems understanding English grammar!

c. Nowadays, getting visas to travel to some foreign countries involves a lot of _____.

d. My father and grandfather both worked in an automobile factory and had _____, but my goals are to be a CEO of a car company and for the company to always be _____.

e. I felt myself getting faint and knew that I would soon _____.

The Social Side of Business

7

Warm Up

Test Your Cross-Cultural IQ

1 In which of these Central American countries is English the official language?
  a. Belize
  b. Guatemala
  c. Panama

2 Juan Rodriguez Garcia, an executive from Mexico, gives you his business card. You should call him:
  a. Mr Juan.
  b. Mr Garcia.
  c. Mr Rodriguez.

3 In Japan, small actions can have great meaning. Which is not an appropriate behavior in Japan?
  a. Bowing to greet people.
  b. Calling your teacher by her first name.
  c. Covering your mouth when you laugh.

4 Match the toast with the country.
  a. Spain   **i.** Kampai
  b. Japan   **ii.** Cheers
  c. United States   **iii.** Salud

5 According to one British tradition, it is good luck if the first person in your house on New Year's Day is:
  a. your grandmother.
  b. a lady in red.
  c. a man carrying coal.

6 True or False: In most Asian countries, the receiver of a gift should not open the gift in the presence of the giver.
  a. True
  b. False

Reading Strategy: Text organization-Compare and contrast

Writers often use a **compare and contrast** structure when writing about two similar but different things. It is easier to understand two separate things by describing their similarities and differences. In describing Australia and South Korea, for example, the writer might explain the holidays, food, and the weather in each country. There are two ways the writer can do this:

• **Block organization**—one paragraph about holidays, food, and weather in Australia, then another paragraph about holidays, food, and weather in South Korea.

• **Point by point organization**—one paragraph comparing holidays in Australia to South Korea, another paragraph comparing food in Australia to South Korea, then a final paragraph comparing weather in Australia to South Korea.

The following words / phrases are commonly used to **compare** information: also, as, as well as, both, in the same manner, in the same way, like, likewise, same, similar, similarly, the same as, too.

To **contrast** information, the following words are often used: although, but, differ, even though, however, in contrast, instead, nevertheless, on the contrary, on the other hand, unless, unlike, while, yet.

Feedback to Warm Up:
1. a; 2. c; 3. b; 4. a-3; b-1; c-2; 5. b; 6. a

Strategy in Focus

1 As you read, decide if the text uses a point by point or block text organization. Underline any words that indicate the organization type.

  a. What is the text about?
  b. What are the most important details?
  c. Why did the author write the text?

An American in China

Ashley O'Brien's intercontinental flight had just landed in Beijing and she was on her way to meet her business colleagues at a banquet. The dinner was to be their first meeting and she wanted to make a good impression. She had spent some time on the plane reading about doing business in China and knew about some of the cross-cultural differences she could expect. First of all, she had read that Chinese names are traditionally written, last name, first name. She also knew being late was considered extremely rude, which is similar to the USA, and that clothing should be conservative.

Since her plane had been delayed leaving New York, she had to go straight to the dinner in her traveling clothes; a nice shirt and pair of jeans. Her book had said that jeans were acceptable in social situations and since this was a dinner, she felt that her outfit would be OK. However, at the dinner she noticed that everyone else was dressed more formally.

She then turned to one of her Chinese colleagues, Xu Yong, and said, "Mr. Yong, it's good to finally meet you. What are your thoughts on my business ideas?" Mr. Xu ignored her mistake with his name and avoiding her question in order to keep the talk over dinner informal, he politely replied, "How was your flight, Ms. O'Brien?"

When dinner officially began and the dishes were being passed around, Ashley was pleased to see a big plate of shrimp as it is her favorite food and was one of the only dishes she recognized on the table. She decided to fill up on that and skip the others. Afterwards, she noticed that unlike her, everyone else just took one shrimp along with a small helping of all the other dishes.

She hadn't eaten much on the plane and was very hungry. She quickly started to eat but when she noticed that no-one else had started, she stopped and waited. She remembered that it would be rude to start a meal before the guest-of-honor had started.

She thought that by cleaning her plate her hosts would understand that she really enjoyed the food. However, at the end of the meal, she noticed that hers was the only empty plate on the table. She realized she had made yet another mistake and then remembered that an empty plate could suggest her hosts did not provide enough food.

By the end of the evening, Ashley worried that she had ruined her credibility and her company's chance to succeed in China. She understood that before she committed any more mistakes, she needed to learn a lot more about doing business abroad.

2 Complete the outline of the case study, "An American in China"

  a. The United States
  i. names: first, last name
  ii. time: _____
  iii. eating: _____

  b. China
  i. names: _____
  ii. time: punctuality is expected
  iii. eating: do not eat everything on your plate

Feedback

1. This text is mainly contrasting information and the following 'contrast' words are used: however, but, instead of, unlike.
2. i. names: last name, first name; ii. time: punctuality is expected; iii. it is acceptable to eat everything on your plate.

Before Reading

1 What is important in making a good first impression at a business meeting in your country? Check ✓✓ = very important, ✓ = important, × = not important. Discuss your answers with a partner.

a. _____ good eye contact   b. _____ dressing in the latest fashion   c. _____ being confident

d. _____ a good handshake   e. _____ being on time   f. _____ smiling

2 Skim the text and decide its main purpose.

a. _____ inform   b. _____ persuade   c. _____ entertain

While Reading

3 As you read, decide if the text uses point by point or block text organization. Underline any words that indicate the organization type.

After Reading

4 Associate the text with your personal experiences. If someone was visiting your country to do business, what should they know about the following:

a. business dress (men and women)

b. introductions (names, handshake / bow / kiss...)

c. attitudes toward time

d. eating

5 Complete the chart.

Information in the Reading 1 text and Strategy in Focus texts.	Information only in the Reading 1 text.	Information from your experience about cross-cultural differences.
a.		
b.		
c.		

6 Highlight:

a. the main idea of the text.

b. where each of the supporting ideas start.

7 Which of these best summarizes what the text is about?

a. The different cross-cultural attitudes about time, introductions, and eating.

b. How to make a good impression when traveling to the Middle East.

c. The importance of knowing about cross-cultural differences when doing business abroad.

Doing Business Abroad

When doing business abroad, it is important to learn as much as you can about your hosts' culture. Positive first impressions are vital to being successful in business and what is accepted in [5] one country may not be acceptable in another. In most countries, good first impressions revolve around knowing the cultural attitudes about dressing, introductions, punctuality, and eating.

A neat appearance is appreciated in all cultures, [10] but some countries have different standards when it comes to dressing. Women have to be especially mindful in some countries. If traveling to the Middle East for example, women should dress in modest, loose-fitting clothes; a high [15] neckline, long-sleeve shirts and a skirt that falls near the ankles. Showing a lot of skin is considered immodest and in poor taste. In China, conservative, muted-color clothing is also more common for both men and women and although [20] jeans might be fine for social situations, they are not appropriate for a formal meeting whereas in some American and European cities jeans may be acceptable business attire. In India, where Hinduism is a popular religion, the cow is [25] revered and leather products may be considered offensive. However, in many European countries, like France and Italy, finely-made leather shoes are an important component of a person's wardrobe.

[30] Introductions and the level of formality also vary widely from country to country. Even if you have had frequent email correspondence in the past, using first names may be considered too informal and impolite in many countries. However, in most [35] American business cultures, first names are widely used, so when doing business abroad, many Americans have lost credibility or respect by using the first names of their international colleagues. Another point of confusion may [40] revolve around a person's name. Hispanic names can be especially confusing to foreigners because most include two surnames. The first surname comes from a person's father, the second from his or her mother. For example, for a man with [45] the name Javier Garcia Corral, Javier is the first name, Garcia is his father's surname, and Corral is his mother's surname. Both surnames may be used in written communication. But only the father's name is commonly used in verbal [50] communication—the person in this example would be addressed as Senõr Garcia or Mr. Garcia.

Attitudes about punctuality also differ depending on the country. For example, being on time is [55] expected in Germany and Japan, where being late may show that you cannot manage your time or keep your word. In the United States and Canada, if you are around five minutes late most people will not be insulted. This differs from Spain, [60] Italy, and most of Latin America, where it may be fine for someone to be fifteen minutes late. In many Middle Eastern and African countries, punctuality is not traditionally valued; people could show up an hour late without it conveying [65] an insult. However, if you come from a culture where punctuality is important, they would expect you to adhere to those standards. For example, if you were a German doing business in Saudi Arabia, you would be expected to be on time.

[70] Finally, most business relationships are improved over meals and most international executives will find themselves sharing meals with their colleagues. Knowing a country's preference for food, topics of conversation, and eating etiquette [75] will help you avoid making some serious cultural gaffes. For instance, some religions have food taboos (pork or alcohol to Muslims and beef to Hindus) so do not serve those foods to visiting executives. Other countries have different [80] attitudes about doing business during meals. For many time-pressed North Americans, it is fine to discuss business over meals, expected even,

continued on page 68

but to the Chinese, meals are primarily a social occasion and therefore not a place to discuss work in detail. It is also important to know dining etiquette. In many African and Middle Eastern countries, it is considered unclean to use your left hand for eating. In the USA it is common for people to eat with a fork held in the right hand while the left is empty. However, in several European countries, it is traditionally considered rude to place your left hand in your lap. Instead, both hands should be visible (even when not eating) and the fork should be held in the left hand and the knife in the right.

It is said that you never get a second chance to make a first impression. Understanding the local culture will give you an advantage in making a good first impression, and when it comes to doing business you want any advantage you can get.

Word Work

8 Make word chunks from the article using the verbs in the box.

lose	vary	keep	do	be

a. _____ your word

b. _____ mindful

c. _____ credibility

d. _____ widely

e. _____ business

9 Choose three chunks and make sentences about yourself or a friend.

a. _____

b. _____

c. _____

Before Reading

1 Quickly scan the text to find names, dates, and numbers. Answer the questions.
a. What is CSR?
b. Who was Anita Roddick?
c. When did The Body Shop's Community Trade program start?
d. When was The Starbucks Foundation established?
e. How much money has The Starbucks Foundation given away?

2 Take two minutes to skim the text. What is the main idea?

While Reading

3 As you read, decide if the text uses point by point or block text organization. Underline any words that indicate the organization type.

After Reading

4 Talk about the article with a partner.
a. In your opinion, should all businesses be socially responsible?
b. Have you ever been to a business run like Starbucks or The Body Shop? What was your experience like?
c. What new information did you learn about Starbucks and The Body Shop?
d. When you buy something, do you think about where the product was produced and whether the workers are getting a fair wage?

5 Complete the outline of the text.

a. **The Body Shop**
i. established in 1976
ii. community outreach: _____
_____

iii. The Body Shop Foundation: started in 1990 and given away more than $16 million

b. **Starbucks**
i. established in: _____
ii. commitment to helping the community: Make Your Mark, Fair Trade Coffee ...
iii. The Starbucks Foundation:
_____

6 Find these words in the reading. Then match each word with its meaning.
a. corporate (line 4)   •   •   i. yearly
b. robust (line 23)   •   •   ii. become successful
c. thrive (line 32)   •   •   iii. strong and successful
d. annual (line 44)   •   •   iv. vital, important
e. integral (line 100)   •   •   v. relating to a large company

Businesses that Make a Difference

In the business world, the main responsibility of corporations has traditionally been turning a profit. However, in the last decade a new focus for corporate social responsibility (CSR) has taken [5] hold, one that places a premium on companies being responsible in the workplace, towards the local community, and the environment.

Although CSR projects are now standard business practice for most companies, this was [10] not the case when the cosmetics company The Body Shop started in the United Kingdom in 1976. However, from the very beginning, founder Anita Roddick believed that her business had to be about public good and social responsibility. This [15] remained important even as her business grew to become a large multi-national company and continued even after Roddick sold the company to a much larger business. As the Body Shop's website explains, "We believe business is about [20] more than just the exchange of products and money. It is about an exchange in experience, community action, and knowledge, too." The Body Shop maintains what it describes as a robust plan of CSR centered on the ideas of supporting [25] community trade, defending human rights, and protecting the planet.

The Body Shop's Community Trade program, started in the late 1980s, was the first of its kind for a cosmetics company. The company now [30] works with suppliers in more than 20 countries and guarantees a fair and reliable wage helping the local communities to thrive. For instance, in Ghana, one Community Trade partner is Kuapa Kokoo, a supplier of cocoa butter used in a body [35] lotion. Through Kuapa Kokoo more than 50,000 small-scale farmers now receive a fair (above average) price for their cocoa butter. The Body Shop's trade also contributes to Kuapa Kokoo's social fund, which is used to provide schools, [40] wells, drinking water, and medical facilities.

In addition to its support of Community Trade, The Body Shop has also established the Body Shop Foundation, a charitable foundation set up in 1990 to which the company makes an annual [45] donation of more than $1 million. The foundation supports charities that work on environmental causes, animal welfare, and human rights issues and it has donated over $16 million in grants. The Body Shop Foundation has helped fund [50] organizations working on education in Zambia, environmental conservation in Romania, as well as domestic violence initiatives across Europe and child trafficking in Asia.

Starbucks, established in 1971, is another [55] company recognized for positive ethical social practices. Even though it has faced strong criticism for some of its business practices, the coffee company has a long history of supporting its own employees and local communities. It has [60] been seen as a leader in providing substantial health benefits to many of its part-time and full-time employees in the United States. In addition, Starbucks encourages its own employees to give back to their communities in its "Make Your Mark" [65] program. This program matches employees' volunteer hours with cash contributions to the local charity ($10 for every hour up to $1,000). In 2006, volunteers logged over 300,000 hours of service in the United States and Canada.

[70] Like The Body Shop, Starbucks has also established a foundation. Its work was initially focused on funding literacy programs in the United States and Canada, but it has since grown to include supporting education and youth [75] leadership programs in communities wherever Starbucks has stores, and supporting social investments in countries where Starbucks buys

its coffee, tea, and cocoa. By the end of 2007, The Starbucks Foundation had given more than [80] $22 million in grants to help benefit communities around the world.

Although The Body Shop might appear to have a stronger community trade component, Starbucks is also trying to strengthen its commitment to its [85] suppliers. Starting in the early part of this century, Starbucks started increasing its purchase of Fair Trade Certified Coffee. Growers satisfying certain criteria receive a higher price for their beans, ensuring that those communities are receiving a [90] fair income. Although this coffee only represents six percent of Starbucks' total coffee purchases, it shows a growing responsibility to the needs of its producers.

Companies like The Body Shop and Starbucks [95] have realized that good business is more than just making a large profit. Instead, they have realized that they cannot make large profits at the expense of people and the environment, and they understand that incorporating corporate [100] social responsibility is integral if they hope to stay competitive with today's younger consumers who are paying more attention to ethical and responsible corporate behavior.

Word Work

7 Change the bold words in the sentence with a word chunk from the text.

a. Most companies are most concerned with **making money** and not with CSR. _____

b. Many workers in America cannot afford to see a doctor because their companies do not provide **medical insurance**. _____

c. I started my business a few years ago and had to lower prices this year in order to **keep my customers**. _____

d. My company also encourages its employees **to contribute** to the community by volunteering. _____

e. When taking a test, it is important that you **take notice of** the directions and read them carefully. _____

8 Choose three chunks and make sentences about yourself or a friend.
a. _____
b. _____
c. _____

Reflection

▶ Which was your favorite text in this unit? Why?

▶ Which reading strategies did you use in this unit?

▶ Which new word chunks will you make an effort to use in the next five days? Choose at least five.

8 People Tell Lies

Homework

Warm Up

1 Match the lie with the picture.
- a. __D__ "This is great. I love it."
- b. __C__ "This is delicious."
- c. __B__ "Don't worry. Annie's parents will be at the party and there won't be any boys."
- d. __A__ "I didn't touch her."

A

B

C

D

Reading Strategy: Text Organization - Logical organization

Recognizing the way a text is organized will help you understand a text. There are various types of text organization such as Time Order, Compare and Contrast, Persuasive, and Cause and Effect.

Many texts also have their own **Logical Organization.** Often the logic is based on themes for example, the text about Color Symbolism in Unit 6 is organized by taking a different color – green, red and blue – as a theme for each paragraph.

We can look at the text about Gender Stereotyping in Advertising in Unit 5 as another example. In each paragraph, the text looks at a different way advertisements stereotype males and females. Each paragraph deals with a new theme. The text first analyses the roles men and women typically play in TV commercials, the text then looks at the differences in the way men and women are portrayed in commercials, similarities in male and female body types in commercials are examined before ending with a section on the gender stereotyping of children. Understanding the organization (male and female roles → how men and women portrayed differently → how male and female bodies are the same → how boys and girls are portrayed in TV commercials) helps you to understand and remember the text you are reading.

Finding the themes in a text is similar to finding the main idea for each paragraph, but a theme may be longer than just one paragraph and is usually bigger than a single idea. For example, in the Color Symbolism text, one of the themes was the color Green. One paragraph explained the meaning green has in different cultures and another paragraph explained how the color green affects people psychologically.

Feedback to Warm Up:
a. D; b. C; c. B; d. A.

Strategy in Focus

1 | Read the text and decide which logical organization is used.

a. example of an urban legend → facts about urban legends → reasons for creating urban legends

b. definition of an urban legend → example of an urban legend → history of the example

c. where you find urban legends → definition of urban legends → different types of urban legends

What is an Urban Legend? *lend*

Urban legends are popular stories that most people believe are true. These stories are spread from person to person in conversations, through emails, and even in school books. Events in urban legends are typically incredible, humorous, heroic, embarrassing, or terrifying. Often these stories include some kind of moral message and they are rarely based in fact—mostly they are completely untrue.

One of the most popular urban legends in America is the story of the country's first president, George Washington, and his father's cherry tree. Most Americans know the story: George Washington was given an axe when he was just six years old. He loved his little axe so much that he spent all day chopping wood with it. One day he accidentally killed his father's cherry tree. His father was angry when he saw the damaged tree and asked young George if he knew what had happened. According to the story, George told his father he could not lie and then admitted to chopping down the tree. George's father was very proud of his young son for telling the truth and was not angry about his tree anymore.

Parents and teachers tell children this story to teach the importance of honesty, but the truth is, it probably never happened. It is more likely that George Washington's first biographer created the story to improve Washington's image.

Feedback

The answer is b. The first paragraph explains what an urban legend is. The George Washington story is used as an example of an urban legend in the second paragraph, and the final paragraph explains how this urban legend started.

The Signs of Lying

Before Reading

1 Look at the title and the picture. What do you think the text is about?

    a. How to tell lies effectively.
    b. The story of a liar.
    c. How to tell if someone is lying to you.

2 Skim the text and check your hypothesis. Underline statements that confirm your hypothesis.

While Reading

3 As you read the text, decide if you agree [✓] or disagree [×] with the interpretations of these underlined phrases.

	Interpretation	✓ / ×
a. "It is said that <u>a person's eyes are the windows to their soul</u>," (line 10)	You can find out a lot about someone's personality by looking into their eyes.	✓
b. "It is also common for a liar to avoid making eye contact altogether for fear of you <u>seeing through the lie</u>." (line 24)	Knowing this is a lie.	✓
c. "Body language is another way to see if <u>someone is telling tales</u>." (line 22)	Telling you a popular story.	×
d. "It seems that when we are being <u>less than truthful</u> our hands want to cover our face in some way." (line 32)	Lying.	✓

After Reading

4 Decide which logical organization is used.

    a. definition of a lie → types of people who lie → reasons for lying
    b. introduction → example of a lie → example how to detect lies → reason for detecting lies.
    c. context for detecting lies → eyes give clues to lies → body language clues → interaction clues → conclusion

5 Relate the text to your personal experiences. Tell a partner:

    a. about a lie you told.
    b. about a lie you think someone told you.
    c. if you think you can tell if someone is lying after reading the article.

The Signs of Lying

Parents can usually tell if their children are lying to them, and so can teachers. Police detectives are trained to question suspects and separate the truth from the lies in order to solve crimes. [5] Knowing if someone is lying can be useful not just to parents, teachers, and the police, but also in business, politics, or even your personal life. There are a number of behaviors that you can observe to help catch someone in a lie.

[10] It is said that a person's eyes are the windows to their soul, but eyes can also provide strong clues to help you decide if you are hearing the truth or a lie. Here is a simple experiment you can try out on a friend or a family member. Ask [15] them to imagine their mother with green hair. You should notice that their eyes look up to their left while they are imagining their mother. Then ask them to think about what they did this morning and their eyes will probably look up to the right. [20] Basically, eye movement to the left indicates the person is imagining something that is not real or did not happen. When the eyes move up and to the right, the person is remembering something that actually happened. It is also common for a [25] liar to avoid making eye contact altogether for fear of you seeing through the lie.

Body language is another way to see if someone is telling tales. A professional poker player will probably tell you not to believe someone [30] whose hands touch their face, throat, or mouth. Scratching your nose or behind your ear are other clues to lying. It seems that when we are being less than truthful our hands want to cover our face in some way. It is also much more likely that [35] a liar will make few large arm and hand gestures, and will instead try to take up less space, drawing less attention to themselves and thereby hoping that their lies go undetected. It is unlikely that a liar will touch their chest (heart) with an open [40] hand.

Paying careful attention to how people talk and interact can also help you catch someone in a lie. If a student is accused of copying a homework assignment, and is guilty, they are likely to get [45] defensive. They may for example, deny the copying and ask why the teacher does not like him or her, whereas an innocent person might be expected to go on the offensive, explaining for example, how they got the ideas for the homework [50] and convincing the teacher to talk to someone who saw them do the homework. In this situation the liar would probably also repeat the teacher's words in answer to the question. When asked, "Did you copy the homework assignment?" The [55] liar is more likely to answer, "No, I did not copy the homework assignment."

continued on page 76

You may also find a guilty person speaks more than is natural and adds lots of unnecessary details to their story in an attempt to convince [60] you they are telling the truth. If you suspect this is happening, try changing the subject of your conversation quickly. A liar will happily follow your change of direction and will become more relaxed.

[65] But remember, just because someone is demonstrating one or more of the signs associated with lying does not necessarily make them a liar. Some other form of stress other than lying may account for their behavior, and some [70] people exhibit these signs as normal behavior. However, if you need to distinguish a lie from the truth, these tips could be a good start.

6 | **Decide if the statements are true (T) or false (F), according to the text.**

a.   T   **F**   Students always tell the truth to their teachers.

b.   T   F   If someone is lying about what they were doing last night, their eyes will look up to the left.

c.   T   **F**   A liar will touch their heart or chest when they are lying.

d.   T   **F**   Students will attack a teacher if they are caught copying their homework assignments.

Word Work

7 | **Write sentences about the text using these word chunks.**

... question suspects ... .
... avoid making eye contact ...
... body language ...
... pay careful attention ...
... guilty person ...
... innocent person ...
... change the subject ...

8 | **Choose three chunks and make sentences about yourself or a friend.**

a. _____

b. _____

c. _____

Before Reading

1 Decide if you agree or disagree with these statements.

	agree [✓]	disagree [×]
a. Most children start to tell lies by the age of 5.		
b. Children learn to lie from other children.		
c. Most adults do not tell lies.		
d. Intelligent children lie less than average.		
e. Children usually lie to avoid punishment.		
f. Most parents believe their children do not lie.		

2 Skim the text and decide its main idea.
   a. Most parents do not know their children lie to them.
   b. Only bad children tell lies and they learn to lie from their friends.
   c. Most children learn to lie from an early age and continue to lie as teenagers.

While Reading

3 As you read the text, check your hypothesis. Underline any statements that confirm your answer.

After Reading

4 Put the themes from the text in the correct order.

   a. _____ introduction   **b.** _____ conclusion   **c.** _____ why kids lie
   d. _____ how kids learn to lie   **e.** _____ how and how often kids lie   **f.** _____ what kids lie about
   g. _____ who lies

5 Complete the chart.

Information in Reading 1 and the strategy in focus.	Information only in Reading 2.	Information from your own experience about lying.
a.		
b.		
c.		

6 Check [✓] the judgments you made and conclusions you drew from the texts in Unit 8.
   a. _____ Lies and false stories can be useful in social situations and as a way to teach.
   b. _____ Everybody lies including parents, teachers, the police, and children.
   c. _____ We should observe children's body language more closely to see if they are lying.

Your Child Probably Lies, Too

Ask someone what their biggest lie has been and you might be surprised to hear stories about their childhood told in great detail as if the lie was told yesterday. However, if you ask someone to
[5] remember when they started to lie, they probably won't have such a clear memory.

New research suggests that most of us learn to lie by the time we are four years old and continue to lie all through childhood. Parents often believe
[10] that lying is a short-lived phase in young children and that often children do not understand the difference between telling the truth and lying; but they would be wrong.

A Pennsylvania State University research team
[15] led by Dr. Nancy Darling found that although almost all of the teenagers questioned thought that trust and honesty are the most important characteristics in relationships and that lying is wrong, 98 percent lie to their parents. It also
[20] seems that academically successful students are just as likely to lie to their parents as students who scored lower in exams. It does not seem to make a difference if students participate in after-school sporting, academic, and club activities either.

[25] Lying seems to be an advanced cognitive and social skill that intelligent children learn faster than the average child. In order to lie, the child must first understand the truth, be able to create a different reality, and then convince others that
[30] their reality is the truth. Very smart kids can

start doing this at the age of two, which can be confusing to parents. They do not know whether to be happy that their two-year-old is showing signs of advanced intelligence or upset that
[35] their kid is lying. Parents may also be concerned about how often their children lie. According to studies observing children at home and school, the average four-year-old tells a lie on average every two hours and this rises to every one and a
[40] half hours by the time they are six.

Less surprisingly perhaps, Dr. Darling's team found that most teens lie to their parents about a number of different topics. Out of 36 topics presented to them, most teens admitted to having
[45] lied about 12 of them. It seems that teens often lie about things such as how they spend their allowance, who they are dating, the friends they are spending time with, the clothes they wear, and how they are spending their social time.
[50] Younger children's lies usually consist of denying bad behavior or telling tall tales (exaggerating or making up stories).

For school children, the most common reason for lying is to avoid punishment. Young children will
[55] deny hitting another child even if the teacher or parent saw the incident, or they will claim to have done their homework even though it would be easy for the parent to check. A child will also lie to avoid disappointing a parent or someone else
[60] in authority, which may also be seen as a way of avoiding a punishment.

One of Dr. Darling's experiments involved secretly observing a child playing a guessing game with one of the researchers. During the game, the
[65] child faced a wall and had to guess what toy the researcher was holding by only hearing its sound. If the child was right three times they would win a prize. The first and second toys, a police car and a crying baby doll, were easy to guess. The
[70] third toy, however, was impossible to guess. The researcher would put a soft soccer ball on top of a musical card making it play classical music. After it became obvious the child could not answer,

[75] the researcher told the child they were leaving the room for a minute and insisted the child did not turn around and look at the toy. Of course, a vast majority of the children (76 percent) looked at the toy before the researcher returned and 95 percent of them lied about it and pretended [80] to guess it was a soft soccer ball, sometimes inventing elaborate and creative explanations for how the music sounded like a soccer ball.

Most parents are shocked to learn that their child could tell such an obvious lie and continue the lie [85] so convincingly. Some of the parents entered the experiment saying their child never lies.

Often parents do not realize that they are the ones who taught their children to lie and gave them the idea that there is nothing wrong in lying. Children [90] usually hear their parents tell at least one lie a day from an early age. These lies range from how great a bad meal tastes to demonstrating friendship to someone they do not like. Children are told time and time again to be happy when [95] receiving presents they do not like and to look interested when they are bored. These ideas send the message that lying can be OK.

Dr. Darling's researchers found that threatening children with punishment for lying does not have [100] any effect on lying, but praising truthfulness does. Some of the children in the experiment were told the story of George Washington and the cherry tree before the test. Almost half of these children later admitted to having looked at the toy when [105] the researcher was out of the room. It seems rewarding honesty may be a better approach than punishing lies.

Word Work

7 Circle the correct word chunk.

   a. I used to love listening to my grandmother's stories about her childhood. She used to go into such **huge detail** / **great detail** I could imagine being there.
   b. I don't have a very **clear memory** / **clean memory** of my primary school but I remember playing lots of games.
   c. My sister began **showing signs** / **giving signals** of musical talent before she was five years old.
   d. My father used to get very angry when I was a child because of my **wrong behavior** / **bad behavior.**

8 Choose three chunks and make sentences about yourself or a friend.
   a. My brother has a bad behavior in school
   b. My parents gave me great detail of their marriages
   c. _____

Reflection

▶ Which was your favorite text in this unit? Why?

▶ Which reading strategies did you use in this unit?

▶ Which new word chunks will you make an effort to use in the next five days? Choose at least five.

9 School Debates

Warm Up

1 Read each statement. Check [✓] those you agree with.

a. _____ Homework should be banned.
b. _____ MP3 players and cell phones should be allowed in schools.
c. _____ School hours should be from 9 a.m. to 2 p.m., six days a week.
d. _____ All students should have to do physical education.
e. _____ Corporal punishment should be banned.
f. _____ School should only be compulsory for students up to 16 years.

2 Choose one of the statements above and think of 3 justifications to support it and 3 arguments against it.

Statement: _____	
For (Pro)	**Against (Con)**
1.	1.
2.	2.
3.	3.

Reading Strategy: Text Organization - Persuasion

Persuasive texts try to convince the reader to agree with the writer's way of thinking. Writers will often use facts that support their argument and might also anticipate what their opponent might say and argue against (refute) it.

For example, School uniforms should be required in all schools because it is more affordable as uniforms cost less than fashionable clothing.

The **supporting argument** is that uniforms cost less than fashionable clothing.

Refuting an opponent's argument may go like this:
Some experts might argue that school uniforms prevent a student from expressing their individuality, but this is not true because students often customize their uniform with a different belt or tie or they can rebel by not tucking in their shirt.

The writer states the opponent's argument and then **refutes** it by explaining why the opponent's argument is wrong.

Strategy in Focus

1 Skim the text once, then check [✓] the statement that expresses the writer's position.

a. _____ Homework is beneficial and necessary for learning.

b. _____ Homework is more harmful than helpful for students.

2 Read the text again. Annotate the supporting reasons that the writer uses to try to convince you of her opinion.

What Good is Homework?

Emily Weis, a senior at Central High School has been hunched over her desk at home for the past hour, busily doing her math homework. She figures that she will be done with everything in about three hours, giving her a little time to watch television before going to bed. "I wish I had time to just hang out or even exercise, but I have to work hard in order to get into a good university. I just cannot afford to relax and have fun," Emily explains. Her situation is not unique; as university entrance requirements become more competitive and federal requirements on school achievement become stricter, more and more students are being overburdened with homework.

Although, many teachers honestly believe that homework benefits students, it can actually be counterproductive. Besides causing serious health problems, it stunts students' enjoyment of learning and has negligible effect on younger students' achievements.

It is no surprise that homework is a major cause of health problems. For one, there is the pressure of completing everything on time, which leads most students to sacrifice healthy activities like sports, which can have serious consequences. If children are spending more time sitting and doing homework, it is more likely that they will become unhealthy. Then there is the stress of living up to parents' and teachers' expectations. The pressure to be 'perfect' leaves students with headaches, stomach aches, and even insomnia. Stress is such a serious problem amongst students in the USA that the American Academy of Pediatrics (2007) cautioned that both stress and depression in children are on the rise and recommended counteracting this with more time for play.

Most students end up resenting rather than enjoying their homework. Instead of viewing homework as an opportunity to reflect on and reinforce what they learned in school, students will often try to rush through one assignment to get to the next one, and finish as quickly as possible. Or worse, because of time and parental pressures, many students might feel compelled to cheat, perhaps copying something from the Internet for a writing assignment or using a classmates' solutions to a math problem.

Although some people believe that homework is beneficial, arguing that the more you practice, the better you become, the detrimental effects of homework far outweigh any potential benefits. In fact, a recent Canadian study has shown that there is no correlation between academic achievement and homework in primary school students. What would be more helpful and less stressful to students would be more supervised study time. At least then students would have access to teachers trained to answer their questions and then be able to leave school and do what kids should do – enjoy their childhood without the stress of homework.

Feedback

1. (b); 2. Annotations will vary but the supporting reasons are: homework is a major cause of health problems (stress and depression are on the rise), students resent homework and do not enjoy learning (might cheat), a study proves there is no correlation between academic achievement and homework in primary school students.

Before Reading

1   **What are some possible reasons to have homework? Check [✓] your answers. Add your own ideas.**

a. _____ It helps students to remember and learn.   b. _____ It prepares students for university study.

c. _____ It is fun.   d. Your ideas: _____

2   **Skim the text. What is the main idea?**

a. The writer believes that homework adds to the stress that is a natural part of adolescence.

b. The writer believes that homework contributes to the academic and personal success of students.

c. The writer believes that homework benefits high school students but should be banned in primary schools.

While Reading

3   **Highlight the arguments and refutations in the text.**

After Reading

4   **Ask a partner questions about the text.**

a. Which ideas do you agree with?

b. Which ideas do you disagree with?

5   **Complete the chart.**

Information in Reading 1 and the Strategy in Focus texts.	Information only in Reading 1.	Information from your own experience.
a.		
b.		
c.		

6   **Decide if the statements are true (T) or false (F), according to the Reading 1 text.**

a.   T   F   Homework is the main cause of stress and depression in students.

b.   T   F   Students in third grade should only have 30 minutes of homework a night.

c.   T   F   Students acquire better study skills if they are assigned homework.

The Wonderful Benefits of Homework

There has recently been a lot of controversy surrounding the efficacy of homework, but as a twenty-year-veteran teacher, I strongly believe in the benefits of quality homework. Besides
[5] preparing students for the academic rigors of university life, it teaches important life skills that will benefit students for the rest of their lives.

Some people argue that homework is causing stress and depression to rise in children. To blame
[10] homework solely for these health problems is a gross misstatement. Adolescence is a time of enormous change and fluctuating hormones. In addition, peer pressures about how you act and dress can make this a stressful time for most
[15] teenagers. These social pressures cause more stress for teenagers than homework. If people are really concerned about the welfare of students, they would spend more time addressing the problem of peer pressure in schools rather than
[20] complaining about homework.

In addition, those who are opposed to homework believe that students end up resenting the time spent instead of enjoying learning. However, homework is not the problem in this case. The
[25] problem is the type of homework being assigned. In most teacher training courses, teachers are not exposed to sufficient research on homework.

If they were, they would better understand that it is the quality not quantity of homework that will
[30] enhance students' learning and their enjoyment. Repetitive worksheets where students memorize historical dates and names or solve math problems over and over again are less beneficial than more creative project-based homework.

[35] Although a recent study by the University of Toronto's Ontario Institute for Studies in Education found no connection between academic achievement and homework in primary school children, I would caution educators
[40] against cutting it completely. These students will eventually be in middle and high school where homework will be assigned. If they have no preparation whatsoever in primary schools, they will have the stress of suddenly trying to adjust to
[45] life with homework later. Instead, primary school educators should remember the rule of thumb in assigning homework – about ten minutes per grade per night, thus a second grader would have only twenty minutes of homework a night.
[50] The important thing is to assign just enough homework to help students learn.

In fact, the potential benefits of homework are enormous, for students and their families. Homework allows parents to be aware of what
[55] their child is doing at school and how well their academic and thinking skills are developing. If they notice that their child is struggling with certain math concepts or taking an unreasonable amount of time completing their homework, it
[60] might be indicative of a bigger problem. Parents can then get additional help for their child or call the teacher's attention to the problem. It also allows parents to be connected to what their child is doing in school. In my experience, most parents
[65] want their children to have more rather than less homework because they understand how it helps to reinforce what the child learned in school and it keeps the child from wasting their time in front of the television or playing video games.

continued on page 84

[70] Finally, and most importantly, homework helps to teach students important study and life skills that will set them up for future success. They learn how to manage their time so that they can accomplish their homework and other activities. They also [75] learn how to be more diligent and disciplined, and they learn to be persistent. At times, they might struggle to complete an assignment, but by working through it, they learn not to give up when the going gets tough. These are skills that will not [80] only benefit them in their academic life but in their adult lives as well.

Instead of seeing homework as the root of all evil as some people would like, we should recognize the inherent benefits of assigning [85] developmentally appropriate homework. Quality homework can help show kids the connection between what they are learning in school, and how it can be applied outside of schools, and it should allow the students to have fun while doing [90] it. Learning should not solely be contained within a classroom; it should be extended to all areas of our lives.

Word Work

7 Complete the sentences with a word chunk from the text. You may need to change the tense. One chunk will not be used.

strongly believe	to address the problem	to learn how to manage their time
an unreasonable amount of time	be indicative of a bigger problem	better understand

a. Many people believe that we need _____ of global warming.

b. Many environmentalists _____ that if nothing is done soon about global warming, the world will suffer from serious consequences such as extreme flooding.

c. Many students need _____ when it comes to writing long research papers.

d. Some students spend _____ thinking about what they write when they should just sit down and write.

e. The rising number of school drop-outs _____ ; that schools are not addressing the bigger problems leading to students leaving school early.

8 Choose three chunks and make sentences about yourself or a friend.

a. _____

b. _____

c. _____

Before Reading

1 You are going to read a text about using MP3 players in school. Read these statements and answer "Yes" or "No."

    a.   Yes / No   Do you have an MP3 player?
    b.   Yes / No   Do you use your MP3 player only for entertainment?
    c.   Yes / No   Do you think MP3 players should be allowed in schools?
    d.   Yes / No   Do you think MP3 players could be used for educational purposes?

2 Before you start reading, mark down the starting time.

    Starting Time: _____

While Reading

3 Read the article quickly and without stopping.

After Reading

4 After you finish, mark down the finishing time. Calculate your reading time.

    Finishing Time: _____   Reading Time: _____

5 The author believes that MP3 players:

    a. should be used in schools.   **b.** should not be used in schools.

6 Check [✓] the type of biases shown in the text.

    a. _____ headline   **b.** _____ photo   **c.** _____ imbalance   **d.** _____ word choice
    e. _____ statistic and numbers

7 Decide if the bold statements in the article are facts [F] or opinions [O].

    a. _____   **b.** _____   **c.** _____   **d.** _____   **e.** _____   **f.** _____

8 Check [✓] the inferences you can make about the text. Underline the statements that help you make the inferences.

    a. _____ Students enjoy using MP3 players to learn.
    b. _____ Professor White is comfortable using new technology.
    c. _____ Some MP3 manufacturers rent out their MP3 players to schools to help poorer students and increase sales and brand awareness.
    d. _____ MP3 players will eventually allow all learning and discussions to be done outside the classroom.

CD 2:
Track 6

Podcasts Revolutionize Learning

Though many adults complain that technology such as cell phones and MP3 players like the iPod are distracting students from learning, more and more people now realize the educational
[5] potential of these devices. Far from being just an entertainment device, MP3 players are revolutionizing the way students learn in schools. (a) **Not only do students get more excited and engaged when using an MP3 player, but they**
[10] **become more efficient learners.**

Georgia College & State University was a pioneer when it came to incorporating MP3 players into the curriculum. (b) **Soon after the iPod was introduced by Apple Computer in 2001, some**
[15] **faculty members began to come up with ways to utilize MP3 technology in their classroom.** Now, MP3 players are used in a multitude of courses ranging from language to history to political science, allowing students to learn in
[20] innovative ways. In Professor Alcarria's Spanish language course, students load MP3 players with language instruction, Spanish music, and Spanish language audio books to help develop their listening skills. Students are also required
[25] to watch authentic Spanish language TV news programs and listen to podcasts (audio files that can be downloaded from the Internet). Meanwhile in Professor White's psychology class on the brain, students' MP3 players are loaded
[30] with information on the human brain and spinal cord. Other resources include a brain dissection video and podcasts related to course topics that students can watch or listen to at any time. In addition, if students have any questions that
[35] come up when studying, they simply email them to Professor White and he records answers via weekly audio podcasts or video vodcasts.

(c) **The teachers who have used MP3 players as a teaching tool are firm supporters of**
[40] **including this new technology in education.** Most believe that they now have much more time in the classroom for introducing complex ideas and discussion. Instead of spending valuable class time by
[45] doing less demanding work like listening to music or watching movies, students can do this on their own and
[50] then come to class prepared for analysis and discussion. Also, the teachers recognize that the MP3 players
[55] allow students to learn at their own pace, which is especially helpful when it comes to learning a
[60] language. Some language students might listen to a podcast or song only once and understand it, while others might need to hear it repeated over and over. In addition, teachers are finding that students are much more engaged in
[65] the material and therefore learning more. Tapping into the technologies that are already an aspect of most students' day-to-day lives has allowed the traditional, passive classroom environment to become much more interactive and creative.

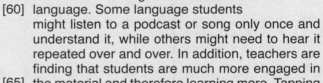

[70] Students who are enrolled in courses that make use of new technology are also happy. Not only do they believe that the MP3 players tap into a more enjoyable way to learn (such as listening to music, watching movies, or podcasting), they
[75] also feel this new technology helps them with their organizational skills and can help save time, too. Audio and text files (such as professors' notes) are sorted and stored in folders that are easy to find and readily accessible. Plus, some
[80] students say they spend more time studying now. As one student put it, "I would never think about opening my textbook and reviewing my notes if I were around people my own age because they would think I was a geek. But, with an MP3 player,
[85] nobody knows I am reviewing my professors' lectures. (d) **It is a much cooler way to learn.**" Others believe that MP3 players also help them become more efficient with their time. "I can listen to my language podcasts or watch course

[90] assigned movies on the bus instead of having to wait until I get home," one student explained.

(e) **Some opponents criticize MP3 players saying they are costly, encourage cheating, and isolate students from each other**. They worry [100] that students might use MP3 players to download notes and use them during exams. Others think that encouraging students to listen to and create their own podcasts takes away from the human element of face-to-face discussion. (f) [105] **They argue that real learning takes place in a classroom and cannot be replicated with MP3 players**. However, this ignores the idea that MP3 players are meant to add to classroom discussion and actually free up time for more face-to-face [110] discussion in the classroom. When it comes to the issue of cost, many schools can loan or rent MP3 players to their students. As for the claim that cheating will increase, teachers simply need to ask students to turn in their MP3 players when [115] taking exams.

Education needs to be responsive to the changing times and technology plays a big part in today's world. Instead of seeing MP3 players as distracting, why not see what they and other [120] technologies can add to the classroom

Word Work

9 Circle the correct word chunk.

a. I have **come up with ways / come with ways** to work less and make more money.

b. I am a **hard supporter of / firm supporter of** allowing cell phones in school.

c. Because I like to **learn in my own pace / learn at my own pace**, I enjoy using computer-assisted language learning programs.

d. I was called to have a **face-on-face / face-to-face** interview for the new job.

e. It is impossible to graduate from college **on today's planet / in today's world** without knowing how to use the Internet.

10 Choose three chunks and make sentences about yourself or a friend.

a. _____ .

b. _____ .

c. _____ .

Reflection

▶ Which was your favorite text in this unit? Why?

▶ Which reading strategies did you use in this unit?

▶ Which new word chunks will you make an effort to use in the next five days? Choose at least five.

Review Reading Strategies

- Unit 7: Compare and contrast
- Unit 8: Logical organization
- Unit 9: Persuasion

1 Which of the above text organizations do these sentences describe? Read each statement and write the answer.

	Text Organization
a. Tries to convince the reader to agree with the writer's opinion.	
b. Organizes information by themes.	
c. Words used in this text organization include "both," "similar," "same," "also," "alike," "unlike."	
d. Refutes an opponent's idea by offering an explanation of why the idea is incorrect or not good.	
e. Describes two similar but different things.	
f. Organizes information in order of importance or interest.	

2 Look at the title and the picture then read the first and last paragraphs of the text. What is the main idea?
- **a.** The problem of online bullying.
- **b.** How to avoid bullying.
- **c.** Why schools need to act now to stop online bullying.
- **d.** Why teens use Internet technology to bully other teens.

3 Read the whole text and decide which logical organization is used.
- **a.** _____ different types of online bullying → facts of online bullying → history of online bullying
- **b.** _____ definition of online bullying → examples of online bullying → facts of online bullying
- **c.** _____ example of online bullying → facts about online bullying → opinions about online bullying → suggestions for stopping online bullying.

4 As you read each paragraph, decide if the bold statements are facts [F] or opinions [O].
a. _____ b. _____ c. _____ d. _____ e. _____

5 Which of these choices best sums up what the text is about?
- **a.** Internet bullying is a teen problem that schools need to handle on their own.
- **b.** Internet bullying is emotionally and possibly physically destructive, and parents, schools, and teachers need to work together to deal with this problem.
- **c.** Internet bullying can affect school relationships and performance in teenagers.

Stopping Online Bullying

[1] An anonymous warning on the Internet bulletin board was posted to a popular eighth-grader at a private school for girls. The author had written, "I feel like throwing up just thinking of you." Messages like that grew more menacing by the day, but it was not until the targeted girl was urged to kill herself that school officials were alerted and intervened, and postings from the much-visited website were deleted. Say hello to cyber bullying or Internet bullying, the newest form of bullying, technologically updated for the 21st century.

[2] The Internet has transformed the landscape of children's social lives. When conflicts arise today, children use their expertise with interactive technologies to humiliate and bully their peers, and often avoid punishment from adults or enemies. Students, parents, and school administrators have all pointed to cyber bullying as the latest, most vicious trend in children's social cruelty.

[3] (a) **About 45 million children in the USA aged 10 to 17 have Internet access, spending hours every day at their computers**. With the click of a button, they can email rumors to scores of recipients for instant viewing, permanently damaging a peer's reputation and social life.

[4] The Internet encourages outrageous behavior in part because it is a gray area for social interactions. Rebecca Kullback, a Montgomery County psychotherapist and former, counselor at a private school in Washington DC, (b) **believes the Internet deletes social inhibitions**. "It allows kids to say and do things that they wouldn't do face-to-face, and they feel like they won't be held accountable in the same way. It gives them a false sense of security and power."

[5] The kids themselves agree. "Emails are less personal," says Elana Lowell, 18, a recent graduate of a Maryland high school. "They're much less formal and more indirect, and it's easier for people to be more honest and even meaner because of that ... It's the same thing when you're talking on the phone because you don't have to face the person directly."

[6] Just as online cruelty may be intensified by the distance separating perpetrator and victim, it also changes the face of bullying itself. "Kids no longer have the safety of being able to go home and escape bullying," Kullback said. "Ten years ago, if a kid got bullied he could go home and sit in front of the TV. (c) **Nowadays, with children spending so much time on the computer, whether to shop, do research for schoolwork, play games, or hang out with friends," Kullback says, "they are easier to target for abuse."**

[7] In most situations school officials disapprove but do little else, arguing that the bullying occurs off school grounds. Yet as every child knows, "juicy" material is quickly passed around, in print or by word-of-mouth, affecting the wider school community.

[8] The best strategy for promoting ethical behavior online may be to take proactive action. Saint Ursula Academy, a girls' school in Ohio, has addressed the problem of online behavior by having students sign an agreement at the beginning of the school year committing them to use the Internet, email, and the school network ethically. Online bullying, if caught, may lead to probation or even dismissal.

[9] Educating school kids about online bullying is just as important as imposing strict rules.

continued on page 90

Most parents would not hesitate to assume responsibility for their child's behavior on a playground, at school, or in someone else's home. What happens online should be no different. (d) **Parents need to pay attention to their child's online behavior and should talk with them about computer ethics, explain appropriate online behavior, and—most importantly—make clear the consequences for bad behavior.** They should instruct their children to never share their passwords and never fight with someone online.

[10] Teachers can also play an active role in instructing children about appropriate online behavior, even where there is no school policy on the issue. By being mindful and promoting public discussion about their lives on the Internet, teachers and students can work together to share advice and develop "rules to type by" or similar Internet-minded guidance. (e) **Schools need to accept the reality of Internet cruelty and review their current policies on bullying.**

Adapted from "Cliques, Clicks, Bullies and Blogs." The Washington Post, with permission from the author, Rachel Simmons, a consultant to schools on psychological aggression and author of "Odd Girl Out: The Hidden Culture of Aggression in Girls" (Harcourt).

Comprehension Check

1 The word "anonymous" in paragraph 1 is closest in meaning to:

a. written
b. unidentified
c. dangerous
d. mean

2 The word "intervened" in paragraph 1 is closest in meaning to:

a. allowed
b. notified
c. became involved
d. asked

3 In paragraph 6, the word "it" refers to:

a. cruelty
b. victim
c. bullying
d. distance

4 The author mentions "develop "rules to type by"" in paragraph 10 as an example of what _____ can do to try to prevent online bullying.

a. parents
b. teachers
c. kids
d. schools

5 Which of the following statements about online bullying is not true, according to the text?

a. Most schools do not have a policy about online bullying.
b. Online bullying could lead to physical harm or injury.
c. It is easier to be mean to someone if you don't have to see them face to face.
d. Kids can go home and escape bullying.

More Word Chunks

1 | Circle the correct word chunk.

a. Some believe that bullying online is easier to do because the bully does not have to be **face to face** / **face on face** with their victim.

b. Parents should **spend attention to** / **pay attention** to their children's online activity.

c. **Bad behavior** / **Bad actions** such as emailing rumors about someone or posting mean messages should be punished.

d. In order to **address the problem** / **direct the problem** of cyber bullying, both schools and parents need to talk to teens and establish rules about online behavior.

e. If everyone **is mindful** / **is minding** of this new form of bullying, hopefully we can cut down on the number of children who are bullied online.

2 | Underline the words which do NOT collocate with the word in bold.

a. **change** _____ :	the subject	of memory	of direction
b. **lose** _____ :	credibility	impatience	business
c. _____ **person** :	bully	innocent	guilty
d. **learn** _____ :	the directions	at my own pace	how to manage my time

3 | In Unit 9, we learned about the word chunk "an unreasonable amount of time" and "manage my time".

I spent an unreasonable amount of time doing my homework last night; six hours is just too much! Many students need to learn how to manage their time better in order to finish all their work and also maintain a social life with friends and family.

Here are some other word chunks with "time" with their definitions:

> time after time (again and again, repeatedly)
> in no time (almost immediately)
> at the same time (however)
> make time for something (to allow time for something)
> kill time (to do something while waiting)
> have a good time (to enjoy one's self)
> run out of time (to have no more time left)
> for the time being (temporarily)

Complete the sentences with a word chunk from the box above.

a. I had an eight hour layover in New York and decided to _____ by leaving the airport and going on a quick bus tour of the city.

b. I always _____ when taking examinations, I get nervous and it then takes me longer to answer all the questions.

c. I would like to see a movie tonight with my friends, _____ my parents have already made plans for us to go to the opera.

d. I am happy with my job _____ , but I know I want to do something else in a year or so.

e. My parents say that college will be over _____ and that I should enjoy studying as much as I can before I have to go out into the real world.

Warm Up

1 Which meal looks the most appetizing to you? Describe each meal using at least three adjectives.

nutritious / delicious undercooked / overcooked	greasy / nongreasy tasty / tasteless	flavorful / flavorless unhealthy / healthy

A

B

C

_____
_____
_____
_____

Reading Strategy: Deducing meaning

Even when reading in your own (first/native) language you might find words you do not understand. However, you would not always use a dictionary to find the meaning of unfamiliar words in a text. Good readers use many strategies to **deduce** (or guess) the **meaning** of unknown words in their first and other languages.

Often you can guess the meaning of words from the context (the situation) you find them in. It is important to read the sentences surrounding the word and to consider the topic when **deducing meaning from context**. For example, if you are reading a text that mentions food staples, you would understand that in this context staples must be related to eating and not the small metal clips used to hold pieces of paper together.

You can also **deduce meaning through co-text**, which means the surrounding words and the way that the word is made up (including prefixes and suffixes). For example, The price of basic staples such as wheat, corn, and rice are at record highs. Such as introduces examples of staples, so you know staples means a basic food item.

You can also **deduce meaning from prefixes and suffixes**. Prefixes (a group of letters placed at the beginning of a word) or suffixes (a group of letters placed at the end of a word) will modify or change the meaning of a word. For example, when the prefix 'un-' or 'non' is added to a word, it means 'not'. So unhealthy means not healthy, nongreasy means not greasy. Knowing commonly used suffixes will also help you identify the word's part of speech (verb, noun, adjective). For example, if you add the suffix –cian to some words (like musician), we can tell it is linked to a person (noun) or if you add –ful to a noun, it changes the word to an adjective.

Strategy in Focus

1 Read the text about competitive eating competitions.

Competitive Eating: Sport or Show?

The competitors are lined up, the starting gun goes off, and the eating begins. Made famous by "Nathan's Famous International Hot Dog Eating Championship" at Coney Island, USA, competitive eating competitions are gaining in popularity around the world. The Coney Island competition attracts around 50,000 spectators and is broadcast around the world. The result of the 2007 competition showed a triumphant Joey Chestnut of the USA setting a new world record by eating 66 hot dogs in twelve minutes, outdoing the six-time hot dog-eating world champion Takeru Kobayashi of Japan. Chestnut again defeated Kobayashi in 2008, but only in extra time after tying in regular time.

Like 'regular' athletes, competitive eaters train for their competitions, working to improve jaw strength and drinking large quantities of water to help stretch their stomach. In addition, and contrary to popular opinion, being bigger is a disadvantage so many of the world class competitive eaters like Kobayashi who weighs only 132 pounds (59.8 kg) are fit and thin. One of the most successful American eaters, Sonya Thomas, is only 105 pounds (47.6 kg). Thin athletes are thought to have a competitive edge because their stomachs are able to expand more since there is little abdominal fat to push against.

Many health advocates oppose calling this activity a sport, believing that it glorifies gluttony and promotes obesity. Some believe that it sends the wrong message to children, that overeating in general and binge eating in particular is fine. However, others disagree. Dr. Brian Wansink, a professor at Cornell University, compares competitive eaters to extreme athletes, "It's the same sort of person who, let's say, would train really hard and compete really hard in a marathon." Wansink also said, "It has the same level of competitiveness and compulsiveness" and added, "One we label crazy and one we label as noble, but in reality it's the same sort of process that drives both these people."

2 Find these words in the story and guess their meaning.

a. international: **i.** between nations   **ii.** confined to one nation
b. outdoing: **i.** work outside   **ii.** perform better
c. disadvantage: **i.** favorable   **ii.** an unfavorable / inferior position
d. overeating: **i.** eat over a table   **ii.** eat a lot
e. disagree: **i.** differ in opinion   **ii.** believe

Feedback:
a. i. the prefix inter- means between / among; b. ii. the prefix out- means to exceed / surpass; c. ii. the prefix dis- means not; d. ii. the prefix over- means superior or excessive; e. i. the prefix dis- tells you that it is a negation of the word 'agree' or to have the same opinion as someone else.

Eating Without Thinking

Before Reading

1 | Based on your own opinion, why do you think people overeat? Check ✓✓ = very important, ✓ = important, × = not important. Compare your ideas with a partner.

a. food packaging   **b.** value for money   **c.** other people
d. plate size / quantity   **e.** depression   **f.** boredom
g. your ideas: _____

While Reading

2 | Circle the images you visualized in your mind while reading the text.

a favorite meal	an office desk with a candy jar	a research lab
people eating soup	people eating popcorn in a movie theater	your dinner table

After Reading

3 | Tell a partner what you saw in your mind as you read the text.

4 | Which of these choices best sums up what the story is about?

a. The emotional reasons why Americans subconsciously overeat.
b. The various environmental factors that influence overeating.
c. How food packaging motivates people to eat more than they should.

5 | Think about the Strategy in Focus text and Reading 1 and complete the chart.

Information in the Strategy in Focus and Reading 1 texts.	Information only in Reading 1.	Information from your own experience.
a.		
b.		
c.		

6 | Put the following words from the text under their part of speech. Underline the suffix that determines each word form.

environmental   subconsciously   boredom   depression   visibility
convenience   workers   another   eating   fullness
mindless   distraction   slowest   mindful   eater

Noun	Verb	Adjective	Adverb

Eating Without Thinking

Dr. Brian Wansink, director of the Cornell University Food and Brand Lab, is obsessed with eating, or at least studying other people's eating behaviors. The author of the book, *Mindless*
[5] *Eating*, examines what environmental factors influence many Americans to subconsciously eat too much.

Many people wrongly believe that physiological factors like hunger or emotional factors like
[10] boredom or depression are the main causes of overeating, but Wansink's research has shown otherwise. "We believe we overeat if the food is good or if we are really hungry. In reality, those are two of the last things that determine how
[15] much we eat," Wansink says. Instead, most people's eating habits are influenced by visibility, convenience, and packaging.

In one experiment, Wansink placed jars of candy in office workers' cubicles for a month. Then, he
[20] moved the candies six feet (1.8m) away. The office workers ate five more candies each day when the jar was close to them, equaling an additional 125 calories a day. It does not sound too bad, but add that up over a year and you will have gained 12
[25] pounds (5.4 kg). "Something that's very visible, every time we see it we have to make a decision. Do I want to eat that? Do I not want to eat that? Do I want that candy on my desk, or do I not want it? We can say no 27 times, but if it is visible, the

[30] 28th or 29th time, we start saying, 'Maybe.' By time 30, 31, we start saying, 'What the heck? I'm hungry," Wansink explains.

In another experiment conducted in his food research lab, Dr. Wansink provided a free lunch
[35] of tomato soup. Unknown to diners, some soup bowls had been rigged to keep the bowl about half full no matter how much soup had been consumed. The idea was to see which would be more likely to make people stop eating: visual
[40] cues, or a feeling of fullness. Diners using the normal soup bowls consumed about nine ounces (226ml) of soup, while the average bottomless -soup-bowl diner ate almost twice as much. Some even continued eating until the 20 minute
[45] experiment was over, finishing more than three times what was in a normal soup bowl! When asked about how much they ate, both groups thought they had eaten about the same amount. Obviously, their perceptions were based on what
[50] they saw left in their bowls, not how they felt.

An extreme example of how packaging can influence a person's mindless approach to eating involved an experiment with buckets of stale popcorn. Moviegoers were given five-day-old
[55] popcorn, some in medium size buckets, some in large buckets. Wansink found that moviegoers who had the larger buckets ate 53 percent more, despite its stale taste. Wansink believes that the distraction of the movie and hearing others eat
[60] the popcorn persuaded people to keep eating.

Wansink's findings in other research have shown that we tend to eat more when we use larger dishes, larger utensils, eat in front of the television, or dine with someone who eats a lot.
[65] Instead of making a drastic change in eating habits, Wansink advocates a gradual approach. People can cut a couple hundred calories a day and lose 10 to 20 pounds (4.5-9 kg) a year by doing things such as avoiding open food dishes
[70] at the office, using smaller serving bowls, sitting next to the slowest eater, and being the last one to start eating. Simple lifestyle changes will add up over time and make you a more mindful eater.

Word Work

7 Match the words to make word chunks from the text.

a. wrongly •   • **i.** a drastic change
b. show •   • **ii.** influenced by
c. to be •   • **iii.** habits
d. make •   • **iv.** believe
e. eating •   • **v.** otherwise

8 Choose three chunks and make sentences about yourself or a friend.

a. _____

b. _____

c. _____

Before Reading

1 Skim the text. What is the main idea?
  a. Rising food prices are causing more and more people to go hungry.
  b. Urgent action is needed if the world is to combat the growing problem of hunger.
  c. Climate change is a key factor in the new face of world hunger.

2 Before you start reading, mark down the starting time.
  Starting Time: _____

While Reading

3 Read the article quickly and without stopping. While reading, decide if your answer to question 1 is correct.

After Reading

4 After you finish, mark down the finishing time. Calculate your reading time.
  Finishing Time: _____   Reading Time: _____

5 Talk about the article with a partner.
  a. I am / am not surprised that ...   b. I think Mr. Ban ...
  c. I think the UN should ...   d. I think world governments must ...
  e. I hope that ...

6 What do you think is the purpose of the text?
  a. To outline the problems that are causing hunger to rise in the world.
  b. To inform readers of the effects that climate change has on hunger.
  c. To persuade people and governments to act immediately to reduce global hunger.

7 Find these words in the text. Then match each word with its meaning.
  a. vulnerable (line 3)   •   •   i.   ruined, destroyed
  b. face (line 10)   •   •   ii. a small amount
  c. staples (line 12)   •   •   iii. weak or easily hurt
  d. devastated (line 18)   •   •   iv. gradually reduces
  e. erodes (line 47)   •   •   v.   have as a prospect
  f. meager (line 48)   •   •   vi. a basic dietary item

CD 2:
Track 9

The New Face of Global Hunger

The price of food is soaring. Hunger and malnutrition is a growing threat. Millions of the world's most vulnerable people are at risk. An effective and urgent response is needed.

[5] The first of the Millennium Development Goals, set by world leaders at the UN summit in 2000, aims to reduce the proportion of hungry people by half by 2015. This was already a major challenge, not least in Africa where many nations have fallen [10] behind, but we now face a perfect storm of new challenges.

The price of basic staples—wheat, corn, rice— are at record highs, up 50 percent or more in the last six months. Global food stocks are at historic [15] lows. The causes range from rising demand in major economies like India and China to climate and weather-related events such as hurricanes, floods and droughts that have devastated harvests in many parts of the world. High oil [20] prices have increased the cost of transporting food and purchasing fertilizer. Some experts say the rise of biofuels has reduced the amount of food available for humans.

The effects are widely seen. Food riots have [25] erupted in countries from West Africa to South Asia. Communities living in countries where food has to be imported to feed hungry populations are rising up to protest the high cost of living. Fragile democracies are feeling the pressure [30] of food insecurity. Many governments have issued export bans and price controls on food, distorting markets and presenting challenges to commerce.

In January 2008, to cite but one example, [35] Afghanistan president Hamid Karzai appealed for $77 million to help provide food for more than 2.5 million people pushed over the edge by rising prices. In doing so he drew attention to an alarming fact: the average Afghan household [40] now spends about 45 percent of their income on food, compared with 11 percent in 2006.

This is the new face of hunger, increasingly affecting communities that had previously been protected. And, inevitably, it is the so-called [45] "bottom billion" who are hit hardest: people living on one dollar or less a day.

When people are that poor and inflation erodes their meager earnings, they generally do one of two things: they buy less food, or they buy [50] cheaper, less nutritious food. The end result is the same—more hunger and less chance of a healthy future. The UN's World Food Program (WFP) is seeing families who previously could afford a diverse, nutritious diet dropping to one [55] staple and cutting their meals from three to two or one a day.

Experts believe that high food prices are here to stay. Even so, we have the tools and technology to beat hunger and meet the Millennium [60] Development Goals. We know what to do. What is required is political will and resources directed effectively and efficiently.

First, we must meet urgent humanitarian needs. This year, the WFP plans to feed 73 million people [65] globally, including as many as 3 million people each day in Darfur. But to do so, the WFP requires an additional $500 million simply to cover the rise in food costs. (Note: 80 percent of the agency's purchases are made in the developing world).

[70] Second, we must strengthen UN programs to help developing countries deal with hunger. This must include support for safety-net programs to provide social protection, in the face of urgent

need, while working on longer term solutions. We [75] also need to develop early warning systems to reduce the impact of disasters. School feeding—at a cost of less than 25 cents a day—can be a particularly powerful tool.

Third, we must deal with the increasing [80] consequences of weather-related shocks to local agriculture, as well as the long-term consequences of climate change—for example, by building drought and flood defense systems that can help food-insecure communities to cope [85] and adapt.

Lastly, we must boost agricultural production and market efficiency. Roughly a third of food shortages could, to a significant degree, be alleviated by improving local agricultural distribution networks [90] and helping to better connect small farmers to markets. UN agencies such as the Food and Agriculture Organization and the International Fund for Agricultural Development meanwhile are working with the African Union and others [95] to promote a "green revolution" in Africa by introducing vital science and technologies that offer permanent solutions for hunger.

But that is for the future. In the here and now, we must help the world's hungry hit by rising food [100] prices. That means, for starters, recognizing the urgency of the crisis—and acting.

Based on a speech given in 2008 by United Nations Secretary General Ban Ki Moon

Word Work

8 Make word chunks from the text, using the words in the box.

a growing	fall	record	perfect
over	widely	draw	

a. _____ the edge   b. _____ attention to   c. _____ highs
d. _____ behind   e. _____ seen   f. _____ threat
g. _____ storm.

9 Choose three chunks and make sentences about yourself or a friend.
a. _____
b. _____
c. _____

Reflection

▶ Which was your favorite text in this unit? Why?

▶ Which reading strategies did you use in this unit?

▶ Which new word chunks will you make an effort to use in the next five days? Choose at least five.

More than a Game

Warm Up

1 List words and ideas that come to mind when you see these pictures. Discuss them with a partner.

27 stns
his hold The flag
Brazilian guy

Fan

ball
World cup

Reading Strategy: Understanding references

Reference words such as she, his, her, himself, those, which, and both usually **refer to** nouns that have appeared earlier in the text and sometimes to nouns appearing later in a text.

For example, "Italy won the World Cup in 2006. It was the second time they had won it. Both teams in the final, Italy and France, had won the World Cup before."

- *They* and *it* replace the nouns *Italy* and *the World Cup*. The writer does not need to repeat *Italy* and *the World Cup* and uses the references *they* and *it* instead.

- The phrase, *Both teams*, refers to *Italy and France*. The words *Italy* and *France* appear later in the text.

Other types of reference are **superordinates and hyponyms.** Superordinates are general words that refer to a group, whereas hyponyms are specific members of the group. Animal, for example, is a superordinate whose hyponyms include words like dog, cat, and elephant. Depending on the context, the writer may go from a superordinate to its hyponyms or vice versa.

It is important to understand what word(s) a **reference** substitutes to understand a text. Identifying the correct word(s) for a reference is also a useful test-taking skill because tests such as TOEFL, and TOEIC, ask questions to test this knowledge.

To find the word(s) a **reference** refers to, read the sentence where the reference appears, and then read the previous sentence or two again. To confirm you have identified the correct word for the reference, substitute the word(s) for the reference. If the substitution is logical, you have probably identified the correct word(s).

Strategy in Focus

1 Read the text and answer the questions related to references.

A Soccer Rags to Riches Story

In August 2008, English newspapers reported that Emmanuel Adebayor signed a new contract with Arsenal FC for $140,000 a week, which is more than $7m a year. However, like most Africans in **the modern game**, Adebayor was born and raised in a desperately poor family.

He grew up in a rundown house in a poor suburb of the Togolese capital, Lome. His mother sold dried fish at the border with Ghana, earning barely enough to feed the family and struggled to buy the promising **athlete** his first pair of soccer boots. The family was so poor that he was once left in hospital for seven days because his parents could not afford to pay for the treatment.

Adebayor once told a journalist, "I put in a lot of hard work to be where I am today, but I will never forget what it was like when I was young. Life was very difficult, and I told myself that I only had one chance to survive and that was to be a soccer player."

a. "... which is more than $7m a year." The word **which** refers to:
- **i.** Arsenenal FC.
- **ii.** $140,000 a week.
- **iii.** a new contract.
- **iv.** $7m a year.

b. The phrase **the modern game** refers to:
- **i.** the Olympic games.
- **ii.** the World Cup.
- **iii.** soccer.
- **iv.** athletics.

c. The word **athlete** refers to:
- **i.** Adebayor.
- **ii.** Soccer player.
- **iii.** African soccer player.
- **iv.** runner.

d. "... he was left in hospital for seven days." The word **he** refers to:
- **i.** Adebayor.
- **ii.** the family.
- **iii.** an athlete.
- **iv.** Adebayor's father.

e. "I will never forget what it was like when I was young." The word **it** refers to:
- **i.** Togo.
- **ii.** playing soccer.
- **iii.** his family home.
- **iv.** life.

Feedback: a. ii, b. iii, c. i, d. i, e. iv

Soccer is Not Always a Rags to Riches Story

Before Reading

1 **Skim the text. What is the main idea?**

a. Professional soccer players can make a lot of money.

b. Young boys from poor countries can play professional soccer in Europe and escape poverty.

c. Criminals in Africa are exploiting young boys by charging large fees for professional soccer contracts that do not exist.

While Reading

2 **As you read, underline any words that support your hypothesis.**

After Reading

3 **As you read each paragraph, decide if you agree [✓] or disagree [×] with these judgments:**

Paragraph 1:   a. _____ It is unrealistic for kids to think they can go to Europe to be rich.

                 b. _____ Governments should protect these kids against the criminals.

Paragraph 2:   a. _____ The police should investigate all soccer academies in Africa.

                 b. _____ Parents should not sell all their possessions to help their children.

Paragraph 3:   a. _____ $1000 is a lot of money in Africa.

                 b. _____ This boy must have been terrified in France on his own.

Paragraph 4:   a. _____ It is more important that the government stop the suffering than get the tax money.

                 b. _____ The reality show to educate young boys is a good idea.

Paragraph 5:   a. _____ Eighty-five percent of soccer players coming from poor families is a surprise.

                 b. _____ It is not a surprise that most of the soccer players lose their money.

4 **Answer the questions about references in the text.**

a. The phrase **these kids** (line 5) refers to:

   i.   African children   ii.   young boys living in poverty

   iii. young boys in South America   iv. heroes

b. Underline the phrase the word **they** refers to.

An increasing number of unlicensed agents and academies have created profitable and unethical businesses out of these desperate boys and their families. For a large fee **they** say that they can introduce a budding soccer talent to a European soccer club.

c. Write down the reference words for **the man**.

The boy's family paid over $1000 for an agent to take him to Europe when he was just 13. After flying to France and arriving at the hotel, he was told the season had started and it was too late to join the club, but not to worry because other arrangements were in place. The boy never heard from **the man** again and now does odd jobs and is hiding from the police.

d. Write down the reference words for **these boys** and the **country**.

Thousands of soccer players are reportedly leaving Nigeria illegally every year. Not only are **these boys** exploited but **the country** is losing out on millions of dollars in tax income from the transfer fees.

Soccer is Not Always a Rags to Riches Story

[1] For kids living in poverty across the world, soccer is more than a sport. From South America to Africa, soccer is often the only hope for young boys and their families to escape poverty. **These kids** see the rags to riches success stories of local heroes such as Diego Maradona from Argentina, Ronaldo from Brazil, Didier Drogba from the Ivory Coast, and Michael Essien from Ghana, and they are desperate for a better life. However, for every Didier Drogba there are hundreds of kids across Africa whose dreams have been exploited and destroyed by a growing number of crooks trafficking vulnerable teenagers to Europe and abandoning them.

[2] In 2008 the BBC reported on unethical soccer academies in Ghana full of young boys all wanting to be the new Michael Essien. An increasing number of unlicensed agents and academies have created profitable and unethical businesses out of these desperate boys and their families. For a large fee they say that they can introduce a budding soccer talent to a European soccer club. Finding the money for the visa, passport, and agent's fee is not easy and the boys' families often sell their homes and possessions in an attempt to fulfill the boys' dreams.

[3] A Cameroonian man in France told the BBC his story was typical of young soccer players who are fooled into believing they will go to Europe and a large soccer club will give them a contract and take care of them. The boy's family paid over $1000 for an agent to take him to Europe when he was just 13. After flying to France and arriving at the hotel, he was told the season had started and it was too late to join the club, but not to worry because other arrangements were in place. The boy never heard from the man again and now does odd jobs and is hiding from the police.

[4] Thousands of soccer players are reportedly leaving Nigeria illegally every year. Not only are these boys exploited but the country is losing out on millions of dollars in tax income from the transfer fees. Justin Fashanu, an ex-England international soccer player and a Goodwill Ambassador for UNICEF, is trying to stop the trend of illegal trafficking by agents who smuggle young, talented players across Nigerian borders in the middle of the night. Fashanu has created a soccer reality show where, for 45 days, 30 contestants will learn about soccer and how to manage their resources.

[5] Fashanu told the BBC that "soccer is not just a game anymore but serious business. Eighty-five percent of soccer players come from poor families and after making huge amounts from professional soccer end up in debt at the end of their career due to reckless living and poor education."

[6] The European Union has expressed concern over illegal and unethical agents trafficking young soccer players out of Africa, and the charity Save the Children is also working hard to inform African families of the dangers of working with these people. However, soccer is an attractive route to a better world for the poor, and stamping out exploitation will be very difficult.

5 Put the following words from the text under its part of speech. Underline the suffix that determines its word form.

living	profitable	trafficking	vulnerable	possessions	reportedly
illegally	millions	trafficking	reckless	education	dangers
attractive	exploitation		*imprudente*		

Noun	Verb	Adjective	Adverb
millions exploitation education dangers possessions	living trafficking	attractive profitable vulnerable	illegally reportedly

Word Work

6 Spot the differences. Underline word chunks that are different from the original text. There are five differences.

For kids living in poor conditions across the world, soccer is more than a sport. From South America to Africa, soccer is often the only hope for young boys and their families to leave their poor conditions. These kids see the rags to riches achievements of local heroes such as Diego Maradona from Argentina, Ronaldo from Brazil, Didier Drogba from the Ivory Coast, and Michael Essien from Ghana, and they are desperate to improve their living conditions. However, for every Didier Drogba there are hundreds of kids across Africa whose dreams have been exploited and destroyed by a growing number of crooks trafficking innocent young people to Europe and abandoning them.

7 Make word chunks from the story, using the adjectives in the box.

| serious | odd | profitable | poor |
| young | huge | reality | |

a. serious business   b. reality show   c. serious jobs
d. young talent   e. huge fee   f. poor education

8 Choose three chunks and make sentences about yourself or a friend.

a. _____
b. _____
c. _____

Before Reading

1 Tell a partner anything you know about soccer, in particular UNICEF and Barcelona.

2 Take two minutes to skim the text. What is it about?

   a. Soccer players from Barcelona are working with the United Nations.
   b. Barcelona is helping UNICEF by having its logo on their soccer shirts and promoting its work.
   c. Soccer clubs and federations are joining forces with the United Nations to help promote UN projects and raise money for the poor.

While Reading

3 Read the article quickly and without stopping. While reading, decide if your answer to question 2 is correct.

After Reading

4 Highlight:

   a. the main idea of the text.
   b. each of the supporting ideas.

5 Answer the questions about references in the text.

   a. Write down the referents for the word **organizations**. (line 14)
   b. Write down the referents for the word **game's**. (line 34)
   c. Underline the word or phrase **their** refers to.
      Three hundred rickshaw drivers in Madagascar were given new bicycle rickshaws improving **their** working conditions considerably.
   d. Underline the word or phrase **The funding** refer to.
      Meanwhile since 2006 the United Nations Children's Fund (UNICEF) and Spanish soccer club Barcelona have had a partnership – initially for five years, which involves the donation of more than $2 million a year from the club and bearing the UNICEF name on the club jersey. **The funding** goes to help children infected with AIDS in Swaziland, which has the highest estimated HIV rate in the world.
   e. Underline the word or phrase **it** refers to.
      "The assistance from Barcelona is a timely investment in the national response to the HIV epidemic," UNICEF Representative in Swaziland, Jama Gulaid said. "**It** is already touching the lives of Swazi children in multiple ways – improving access to prevention, rapid diagnosis of HIV, life-skills education through sports, birth registration, water, and sanitation."
   f. Underline the word or phrase **its** refers to.
      Didier Drogba of the Cote d'Ivoire acts as a UNDP Goodwill Will Ambassador involved in **its** Stand Up Against Poverty campaign.

CD 2:
Track 11

How Soccer Can Make a Difference

THE MATCH AGAINST POVERTY
Ronaldo & Friends vs. Zidane & Friends

"The power of soccer is a key tool in development and in advocating for the fight against hunger and towards the achievement of the first Millennium Development Goal (MDG) – to reduce by half the
[5] proportion of people who suffer from hunger and poverty in the world by 2015," the United Nations Food and Agriculture Organization (FAO) said in a news release.

The more than 900 soccer clubs that are members
[10] of the Association of the European Professional Soccer Leagues (EPFL) joined with the FAO in 2008 to support its efforts to combat hunger and advance humanitarian causes throughout the world. The **organizations** believe that the
[15] high profile soccer enjoys can be used to draw attention to the plight of the more than 850 million hungry people around the world and can help raise funds to support FAO projects helping poor communities to produce their own food.

[20] The FAO has a similar agreement with the Confederation of African Soccer, which has committed to promote a number of joint initiatives through its member clubs and professional players. The aim is to support the development
[25] of agriculture, and launch educational campaigns related to nutrition and the environment. With this strategy, the two organizations hope that soccer will help promote humanitarian causes with the ultimate goal of improving living conditions for the
[30] world's poorest people.

Another UN agency, the United Nations Development Program (UNDP), has also involved soccer stars in its fight against poverty. Since 2003 some of the **game's** biggest stars
[35] have taken part in an annual match, The Match Against Poverty. World Cup winners, Ronaldo and Zidane, captained the two teams in the fifth match, which was held in 2007 in front of 30,000 spectators. The proceeds from the games help
[40] to finance projects designed to fight poverty in Africa, Latin America, Asia, and in emerging Eastern Europe.

The projects supported by money raised in this way include providing school equipment for 3,000
[45] children in Haiti, building a health center and a school in the Democratic Republic of the Congo, creating 350 construction jobs in Sri Lanka to build washing areas, public toilets, and clean water systems, as well as opening a training
[50] center for young, blind people in Ethiopia. Small businesses in Comoros, Guinea Bissau, Namibia, and Colombia have also benefited from financing and training, and in one project, three hundred rickshaw drivers in Madagascar were given
[55] new bicycle rickshaws improving **their** working conditions considerably.

Meanwhile, since 2006 the United Nations Children's Fund (UNICEF) and Spanish soccer club Barcelona have had a partnership – initially
[60] for five years – which involves the club donating more than $2 million a year and sees the club including the UNICEF name and logo on the club jersey to promote the projects being supported. **The funding** goes to help children infected with
[65] AIDS in Swaziland, a country with the highest estimated HIV rate in the world.

"The assistance from Barcelona is a timely investment in the national response to the HIV epidemic," UNICEF Representative in Swaziland,
[70] Jama Gulaid said. "**It** is already touching the lives of Swazi children in multiple ways, improving

access to prevention, rapid diagnosis of HIV, life-skills education through sports, birth registration, water, and sanitation." UNICEF workers in [75] Swaziland have also used the funds to buy laboratory equipment for testing blood samples and drugs for HIV treatment. Twenty-three new Neighborhood Care Points were also established to help protect more than 1,000 orphans and [80] vulnerable children.

Individual soccer players are also involved in bringing public attention to some of the world's most serious problems. Didier Drogba, a native of the Cote d'Ivoire, acts as a UNDP Goodwill [85] Will Ambassador and is involved in **its** Stand Up Against Poverty campaign. English soccer legend and famous father, David Beckham, acts as a Goodwill Ambassador for UNICEF. On one visit to Sierra Leone he urged the world not to [90] turn a blind eye to the thousands of children that die every day from preventable diseases.

"In Sierra Leone, one in four children dies before reaching their fifth birthday," Beckham said, adding, "It's shocking and tragic, especially when [95] the solutions are simple. Saving these children's lives is a top priority of UNICEF."

Soccer clubs, players, and supporters are recognizing that they can help improve and even solve some of the problems of the world's [100] neediest people. The real hope is that their help won't be necessary in the near future.

Word Work

6 Write sentences about the text using these word chunks.
... draw attention ... *When president Tromp come to ny he will draw a lot attention*
... raise funds ... *Next week I will have a party to rouse funds for cheuty*
... living conditions ...
... public toilets ... *The public toilets are so dary*
... clean water ...
... serious problems ...
... turn a blind eye ...
... a top priority ...
... in the near future ...

7 Choose three chunks and make sentences about yourself or a friend.
a. _____
b. _____
c. _____

Reflection

▶ Which was your favorite text in this unit? Why?

▶ Which reading strategies did you use in this unit?

▶ Which new word chunks will you make an effort to use in the next five days? Choose at least five.

12 Economic Matters

Warm Up

1 Identify as many countries as you can on the map, and match them to the group to which they relate.

Spain
Germany
Iceland
Morocco
The USA
Nigeria
Canada
South Africa
Argentina
Mexico
Brazil
Saudi Arabia

France
Iraq
Sweden
Korea
India
Egypt
Australia
Japan
Russia
Indonesia
Vietnam
China

Africa _____

America _____

Asia _____

Europe _____

Oceania _____

2 How else can you group countries together?

Reading Strategy: Exam practice (Charts / Diagrams)

Many students have to prepare for standardized English language tests like TOEFL ibt and IELTS. Reading comprehension questions are a component of both tests. In addition to testing all the other reading strategies covered in A Good Read, readers will be asked to answer **complete-the-chart** / **label-a-diagram** questions. Even good readers who are not preparing for an examination will find it helpful to use charts and diagrams in their note-taking skills.

These questions require a general understanding of the entire passage or sections of it. In a **complete-the-chart question**, readers are given a list of answer choices and a simple chart and are asked to place the answer choices into the correct categories to complete an outline of the reading. In a **label-the-diagram question**, readers are required to label numbered parts of a diagram related to a description contained in the reading passage.

Feedback to Warm Up: 2. You could group countries by for example, developed/developing/undeveloped status; rich/poor/industrial/agricultural; by climate; or population density.

Strategy in Focus

Measuring Wellbeing:

Gross Domestic Product (GDP) (per capita)

The GDP of a country is one of the ways of measuring the size of its economy. GDP is the total market value of all goods and services produced within a given country in a given period of time (usually a calendar year).

To compare countries of different sizes GDP may be divided by each country's average population to give a GDP per capita (per person)

Top 5		Bottom 5	
1. Luxembourg	$104,673	175. Guinea-Bissau	$206
2. Norway	$83,922	176. Liberia	$195
3. Qatar	$72,849	177. Democratic Republic of Congo	$166
4. Iceland	$63,830	178. Burundi	$128
5. Ireland	$59,294	179. Zimbabwe	$55

Data collected from the members of the International Monetary Fund for 2007.

Human Development Index (HDI)

The HDI measures a country's average achievement in three basic dimensions of human development: health, knowledge, and standard of living. Health is measured by life expectancy at birth; knowledge (education) is measured by a combination of the adult literacy rate and the number of students enrolled in primary, secondary, and tertiary schools; and standard of living is judged by GDP per capita.

For 2007, the United Nations found the following countries to be in the top five of the HDI: Iceland, Norway, Australia, Canada, and Ireland while Mali, Niger, Guinea Bissau, Burkina Faso, and Sierra Leone were ranked at the bottom of the 177 nations that were reported.

1 Check [✓] the countries that were mentioned in both the GDP and HDI lists.
- **a.** _____ Canada
- **b.** _____ Iceland
- **c.** _____ Guinea Bissau
- **d.** _____ Zimbabwe
- **e.** _____ Norway

2 Which of the following are measured by the HDI?
- **a.** _____ Life expectancy at birth
- **b.** _____ Total value of all goods
- **c.** _____ The size of a country's economy
- **d.** _____ Standard of living
- **e.** _____ Number of students enrolled in primary school
- **f.** _____ Adult literacy rate and school enrollment

Feedback: 1. = b,c,e – Canada was mentioned only in the HDI list and Zimbabwe was only mentioned in the GDP list. 2. = a,d,f – the other answers either describe GDP or are incomplete measures of HDI.

Before Reading

1 **Do you agree with the following statements?**
a. Cell phones make peoples' lives easier.   Yes / No
b. Cell phones are distracting and disturbing.   Yes / No
c. Cell phones give people more free time.   Yes / No
d. It is important to have a cell phone for emergencies.   Yes / No
e. It is important to have a cell phone to stay in touch with friends.   Yes / No

While Reading

2 **Circle the images you visualized in your mind while reading the text.**

a bank   a fisherman on a boat   an African using a cell phone

elephants   yourself using a cell phone   a rural village

After Reading

3 **Associate the text with your personal experiences. Tell a partner:**
a. if you own a cell phone and what you use it for.
b. one interesting or surprising fact you learned from the text.
c. if you agree that, "the cell phone is the most transformative technology for development."

4 **Match the phrases below to the correct group.**

a.	High fees
b.	Proof of income not required
c.	Inexpensive
d.	Requires proof of address
e.	Is available to more people

Cell Phone Banking	Traditional Banking
Proof of income not required	High fees
Inexpensive	

5 **Choose three statements that best complete the summary of the text.**
The article, explains how cellular technology is improving African's lives. It describes how ...
a. cell phones help many to increase their productivity and profits.
b. fishermen in Zanzibar use cell phones to find the best market prices for their catch.
c. most Africans cannot afford to use traditional banks.
d. many Africans now have access to financial services thanks to cellular technology.
e. cell phones have improved many Africans' access to health care services.

CD 2:
Track 12

How Cell Phones are Changing Africa

Telephones have come a long way since Alexander Graham Bell invented the first one in 1876. Once used primarily to communicate with family and friends and conduct business, [5] cell phones are now commonly equipped with a camera, computer software, video games, and portable music players transforming them into entertainment devices. Although these extra functions are appealing, the real value of cell [10] phones is in how they can make people's lives better around the world. This can plainly be seen in developing countries where phone access has transformed the way people work, bank, and live.

[15] Africa is currently the world's fastest-growing cell phone market. From 1999 through 2005, the number of cell phone subscribers in Africa jumped from 7.5 million to about 100 million. There are many reasons for this dramatic increase [20] including cheaper costs, easier maintenance, and better reliability especially compared with traditional phone lines. And cell phones, unlike regular telephones using landlines, do not require customers to have a permanent address. [25] Improved access to communication has made a dramatic improvement to living standards, boosted personal incomes, and made local economies much more efficient.

In the Kenyan village of [30] Murgula, Grace Wachira runs a small business knitting sweaters. Before cell phones arrived she had to walk a few hours to the nearest town to [35] buy yarn or see customers that she hoped would be there. Now she calls the yarn shop to arrange for delivery and communicates with buyers beforehand. "I'm saving time, I'm [40] saving money," she says. On the island of Zanzibar, off the coast of Tanzania, a fisherman, Omar Abdulla Saidi, uses his phone to look for a port where he can sell his fish for the largest profit. And in South Africa, wildlife researchers [45] use cell phones in weatherproof cases to help track elephants, cutting the cost of tracking them by up to 60 percent. Cell phones have helped a lot of different workers save time, allowing them to be more productive in their work and life.

[50] Cell phones can be used for more than just talking. They are also being used to offer financial services to millions of poor people who were previously cut off from traditional banking services. In many parts of Africa, full-service banks are often just [55] found in cities. They have high fees, and require proof of address and income in order for people to open an account. In fact, only 20 percent of Africans use traditional banks. Cell phones, however, are making banking-type services [60] available to many more people. For instance in Kenya, people can now transfer money through M-Pesa agenta – pesa is Swahili for money. Cash is given to one agent who will send a code number by text message to the recipient which [65] can be used to get cash from their local M-Pesa

continued on page 112

agent. Other innovative financial ideas have seen people using prepaid phone cards as a way of transferring money.

Not only can cell phones improve people's [70] economic status, but they can also save lives. Many rural workers for example might call for an ambulance or to check to see if a doctor is available before making the long trek to the closest clinic. In rural Uganda, a doctor might [75] use his cell phone to request medical information from a better-equipped hospital in the city. In Kenya, people can use text messaging to ask anonymous questions about subjects like AIDS, breast cancer, and diseases which are culturally [80] taboo topics.

According to Columbia University economist Jeffrey Sachs, "The cell phone is the single most transformative technology for development" enabling remote communities who would normally [85] be shut off from economic opportunities to participate in the market place. As many Africans are proving, cell phones are vital to improving lives.

Word Work

6 Correct the mistakes in these word chunks.

standing rate

a. The **living rate** in Iceland must be very high because they ranked first in the UN's HDI list.
The living rate in Brazil is 82 years

b. Many people use their cell phones while driving **to put aside time**, but this is a very dangerous habit.
We need to put aside time to clean the pool ⟶ SAVE Time

c. My dream is to one day **do a business** that is highly profitable. ⟶ started a business

d. I was eighteen when **I started my first bank account** and deposited my first paycheck. ⟶ open

e. In Kenya, people can use **text sending** to ask anonymous questions. ⟶ text messager

7 Choose three chunks and make sentences about yourself or a friend.
   a. _____
   b. _____
   c. _____

Before Reading

1 Skim the text. What is the main idea?
   a. The life and work of Nobel Peace Prize winner, Mohammed Yunus.
   b. Laxmi Priya, a Sri Lankan businesswoman who received microcredit.
   c. How microfinance works to offer economic opportunities to the poor.

While Reading

2 Read the article quickly and without stopping. While reading, decide if your answer to question 1 is correct.

After Reading

3 Decide if the bold statements in the text are fact (F) or opinion (O) according to the text.
   a. F   **b.** F   **c.** ____   **d.** ____   **e.** O

4 Find these words in the reading. Then match each word with its meaning.
   a. shunned (line 12)
   b. vendor (line 22)
   c. disillusioned (line 41)
   d. lend (line 57)
   e. illiterate (line 93)

   i. seller
   ii. unable to read or write
   iii. avoided evitado
   iv. disappointed or dissatisfied.
   v. to give for temporary use

5 Complete the flow chart below.

The Grameen Bank Lending Model

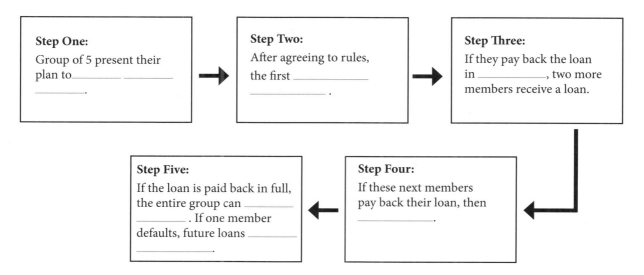

Step One:
Group of 5 present their plan to _____ _____.

Step Two:
After agreeing to rules, the first _____ _____.

Step Three:
If they pay back the loan in _____, two more members receive a loan.

Step Four:
If these next members pay back their loan, then _____.

Step Five:
If the loan is paid back in full, the entire group can _____ _____. If one member defaults, future loans _____.

Fighting Poverty with Microfinance

Laxmi Priya, a Sri Lankan woman, is busily frying snacks to sell on the streets of Colombo. Though she is not rich, her business and her family's lives are much better as a result of
[5] a small loan she received from Grameen bank. Using the loan, she was able to buy a gas cooker and has money to employ one person.

(a) **Microcredit, is a term generally used to**
[10] **describe small loans, often $100 or less, to the poor people who have traditionally been shunned by commercial banks**. Considered a high credit risk because they are often uneducated and unable to provide
[15] any collateral such as property or other assets they could sell if necessary to repay their loan, this population is typically ignored by financial institutions. Microcredit lenders on the other hand target this population to
[20] help them start or expand money-making businesses, such as farming, clothing, weaving, or food vendors like Ms. Priya. The idea is that if the poor have access to credit to start or expand businesses, they will be able
[25] to help lift themselves and their families out of poverty.

The idea of microfinance, which provides the poor with simple financial services such as banking (including microcredit) and insurance
[30] policies, is now a worldwide phenomenon. (b) **It is estimated that almost 68 million people benefit from microfinance institutions in over 100 countries**. Professor Mohammed Yunus is credited with starting this trend over
[35] 30 years ago in Bangladesh.

Bangladesh, at that time, was recovering from intense flooding and famine that had killed at least 40,000 people and over 80 percent of the population was living in poverty. Professor
[40] Yunus, teaching economics at Chittagong University, became disillusioned with the economic theory that he was teaching. As he puts it, "How could I go on telling my students make-believe stories in the name of
[45] economics?" Instead of continuing with the standard economic model that he no longer believed in, Yunus decided to go into the surrounding villages to learn first hand what was maintaining the poverty. Thus he realized
[50] it was an inability to borrow money or receive credit which held many villagers in poverty. Yunus decided to experiment by lending $27 of his own money to 42 women involved in the making of bamboo stools.

[55] From this small venture, Yunus founded the Grameen Bank in 1983. (c) **The bank finds it is better to lend money primarily to poor women as they have been found to typically invest more money back into**
[60] **their family than men would**. The bank's lending model is unique in that borrowers must organize themselves into a group of five and present themselves and their plans to the bank. After agreeing to the bank's rules, the
[65] first two members of the group receive their loan. If, after four to six weeks, they are able to repay loans, then the next two members are offered their loans. If those two are able to successfully repay their loans after four
[70] to six weeks, then the last person is offered a loan. If all five members repay their loan, they are then allowed future credit. However, if any of the members default, then the entire group is denied access to future credit. In
[75] addition, Grameen borrowers are organized

continued on page 115

into centers of eight (eight groups of five) and repayment is collected during weekly public meetings. Thus, any borrower who defaults on a loan is visible to the entire community.

[80] In a country where there is a strong societal pressure to be successful and not bring shame to a family or group, this group lending or joint liability lending model works very well.

(d) **Proponents of microcredit believe**
[85] **that it provides a way for populations to break out of poverty.** Studies have suggested that microcredit also increases women's participation in decision making, reduces domestic abuse, and improves
[90] household nutrition and children's educational opportunities. Yunus cites a favorite example of the power of microcredit when he tells the story of one illiterate Bangladeshi mother who
[95] received a loan, "You look at the mother, that illiterate woman who borrowed money to raise chicken, to buy a cow, to send the daughter to school, and now the daughter is a doctor. (e) **And I get the question in my mind: the mother could have been a doctor, too.**"

[100] Thanks to Yunus's and Grameen Bank's vision, which the Nobel Committee recognized with the Nobel Peace Prize in 2006, millions of people now have a better opportunity to fight poverty and make their lives better.

Word Work

6 Rewrite the sentences using the word chunks below. Change the tense when necessary.

be unable to provide	financial institution	learn firsthand
be denied access to	bring shame	

a. My parents **couldn't give** me money for college tuition, but luckily I received scholarships that helped me financially. was unable to provide

b. I was also able to get a loan from a **bank** which helped with college costs. financial institution

c. Living in another country allows people to **experience personally** what it feels like to be an outsider. learn firsthand (aprender em primeira mão)

d. Because I wasn't wearing proper attire, I **wasn't allowed into** the nightclub. was denied acess to

e. In many cultures, family honor is very important and **causing disgrace** to a family's name is a big offense. bring shame (Trazer vergonha)

7 Choose three chunks and make sentences about yourself or a friend.
a. _____
b. _____
c. _____

Review Reading Strategies

- Unit 10: Deducing meaning
- Unit 11: Understanding references
- Unit 12: Exam practice (Charts / Diagrams)

1 | Which of the above reading strategies do these sentences describe? Read each statement and write the answer.

	Reading Strategies
a. Looking carefully at the co-text and context may help with this strategy.	*Deducing meaning*
b. Superordinates and hyponyms are types of these.	
c. A word that replaces a noun that appears earlier or later in the text.	
d. When taking notes, it may be helpful to organize it with these.	
e. Prefixes and suffixes may help a reader comprehend unknown words.	*Deducing meaning*

2 | Scan the text for numbers and information. Answer these questions.
  a. How many people are infected by malaria each year? *350-500 million*
  b. What is the name of the mosquito that transmits malaria? *Anopheles*
  c. How long is the incubation period of malaria? *7 to 10*
  d. What does IRS stand for? _____

3 | Find these words in the text and deduce their meaning.
  a. sub-Saharan: **i.** located under the Sahara   **ii.** inside the Sahara
  b. unsuspecting: **i.** under suspicion   **ii.** not aware
  c. unable: **i.** not rich   **ii.** cannot
  d. anti-malarial: **i.** against malaria   **ii.** for malaria
  e. decrease   **i.** go down   **ii.** go up

4 | Write down three referents for the word mosquito (paragraph 2).
  a. _____
  b. _____
  c. _____

Malaria

[1] Malaria is one of the world's most common tropical diseases; it infects 350-500 million people every year and kills about a million people annually. It is widely seen in sub-Saharan Africa, where half of all patients admitted to hospital have the disease. Children and pregnant women suffer the most, and recent estimates indicate that a child dies every 30 seconds due to the disease. Although malaria can be controlled, sub-Saharan Africa, Southeast Asia, and parts of the Americas struggle to do so. In fact, in some of those areas, malaria infections seem to be reaching record highs as some strains become drug resistant.

[2] The transmission of the malaria parasite infecting humans is a complex process. When the female mosquito, **Anopheles**, bites a human, **it** transmits cells called sporozoites into the human's bloodstream. These then travel to the liver and each one splits into two new cells called merozoites. After growing and **multiplying** in the liver, these new cells enter the bloodstream and infect healthy red blood cells, where the parasite continues to grow and eventually causes the blood cells to burst. Some of the merozoites develop into sex cells, which are known as male and female gametocytes, and when another mosquito bites the infected human, the mosquito ingests these gametocytes. The male and female gametocytes unite to form a zygote, which after 10–18 days multiplies to form sporozoites. The new sporozoites then travel to the mosquito's salivary glands and when the mosquito bites another human, the entire cycle begins again.

[3] Someone infected might not realize it for a number of days because there is a 7–30 day incubation period before the first symptoms appear. The classical malaria symptoms may consist of three stages that last for about 6–10 hours. The first stage, the 'cold stage', involves feeling cold and shivering, but is followed by a 'hot stage' where the infected person may experience a fever, headaches, vomiting, and seizures. Finally, a 'sweating stage' occurs, where the infected host's body sweats to return to normal body temperature. The sweating is accompanied by extreme fatigue. These stages are repeated every other day or every third day depending on the strain of malaria.

Usually, most patients exhibit a combination of the above symptoms, which to unsuspecting doctors may seem like a severe cold or flu. However, malaria may take even more severe forms if the patient lacks or has depressed levels of immunity to malaria, and it could result in serious problems such as severe seizure, coma, heart attack, kidney failure, and even death.

[4] If detected early, malaria is easily treated with anti-malarial drugs. The type of drug and length of treatment depends on the type of malaria, where the person was infected, their age, if they are pregnant, and how sick they are when treatment begins. Artemisinin-based combination therapies (ACT) are currently the most effective drugs available for treating malaria because few strains of malaria are resistant to these drugs. However, despite the success of ACT, many local hospitals are unable to provide it because of its expense compared to more traditional but less effective anti-malarial drugs.

[5] ACT is also used in pregnant women to help prevent malaria. Other proactive measures can also be taken to decrease the rate of malarial infections. One easy solution is to use insecticide-treated bed nets which families sleep under at night, when the vast majority of transmissions occur. Studies show that these can reduce malaria by as much as 90 percent in areas if many families are using them. Another effective treatment is the spraying of insecticide on the inside walls of a house, a process called Indoor Residual Spraying. This kills the female mosquitoes and helps to reduce transmission to others.

[6] In order to effectively control malaria in the 82 countries that are hardest hit by the disease, it would cost an estimated 3.2 billion dollars annually. A small cost when one considers that malaria costs the African continent about 12 billion dollars a year due to lost productivity and medical costs. It is in the best interest of the international community to pitch in and make battling malaria a top priority.

5 Complete the diagram showing how malaria is transmitted.

A. An _Anopheles_ mosquito bites a human.
B. Sporozoites travel to the liver.
C. Sporozoites _split_ into merozoites and multiply.
D. Merozoites _infect_ healthy red blood cells.
E. Some merozoites _develop_ into gametocytes.
F. Another mosquito bites the _infected_ human and ingests gametocytes.
G. This newly infected mosquito bites another human, spreading the disease.

Comprehension Check

1 The word "multiplying" in paragraph 2 is closest in meaning to:
   a. dividing   b. increasing   c. decreasing   d. lessening

2 Which of the following is NOT a way to reduce malaria mentioned in the text?
   a. indoor residual spraying   b. vaccinating children
   c. using insecticide treated bed nets   d. treating pregnant women with ACT

3 In paragraph 2, the word "it" refers to:
   a. parasite   b. humans   c. process   d. mosquito

4 The author mentions experiencing a fever or headache in paragraph 3 as an example of how malaria:
   a. can be treated.   b. can be deadly to a person's health.
   c. may impact a person's health.   d. may affect children.

5 In paragraph 6, the author implies that many countries are:
   a. not currently doing enough to fight malaria.   b. making money coming up with new malarial drugs.
   c. wasting money on malaria treatments.   d. not affected by malaria.

More Word Chunks

1 Change the bold words in the sentence with a word chunk from the text.
   a. Tropical diseases like malaria are not **commonly noticed** in countries that have temperate climates like Canada and England. _____
   b. During the heat wave this summer, the city experienced temperatures in **unbefore seen numbers** which resulted in many people feeling hot and uncomfortable. _____
   _____

c. Malaria results in **significant troubles** not only for people but for the economies of affected countries.

serious problems

d. Some parents living in extreme poverty **cannot give** their children adequate care and might choose to give their children up to adoption in the hopes of a better life for them.

unable to provide

e. A **leading concern** for scientists studying malaria is finding effective drug therapies that will treat infected patients.

---

2 | Match the words to make word chunks from Units 4, 5, and 6. Then choose a word chunk and write a sentence about yourself or someone you know.

a. poor   **i.** amounts
b. clean   **ii.** institution
c. financial   **iii.** threat
d. a growing   **iv.** water
e. huge   **v.** education

---

3 | In Units 11 and 12 we learned about the word chunks "living in poverty," "living conditions," and "living standards."

The living conditions in many malarial-affected areas are poor due to the fact that many families are living in poverty. Because of this, if we were to travel to such areas, we would probably find living standards quite different from ours.

Here are some other word chunks with "living" with their definitions:

living large	able to pay for and enjoy an expensive standard of living
living the good life	living with a high standard of living
in living memory	able to be remembered by people who are alive now
scare the living daylights (out of someone)	frighten someone
cost of living	the average costs for life's essentials; food, shelter, clothing
make a living	work one does to pay for the essentials, food, shelter, etc.

Complete the sentences with a word chunk from the box. Change the tense if necessary.

a. When she jumped out and shouted, it _____ out of me.

b. I _____ teaching English and tutoring students for the exam.

c. The _____ in New York, London, and Tokyo is very high because they are all very desirable cities to live.

d. Jacob, a successful stockbroker, was eating out every night at a fancy restaurant, living in a luxury apartment building, and was able to buy new clothes every week. He was _____ until the stock market crashed and he lost all his money.

e. That was probably the biggest earthquake _____.

Vocabulary Index

UNIT			Page
abdominal	/ˈæbdɒmɪnəl/	ADJ Abdominal is used to describe something that is situated in the abdomen or forms part of it.	93
accomplish	/əˈkɒmplɪʃ/	V-T If you accomplish something, you succeed in doing it.	33, 83
adolescence	/ˌædəˈlɛsəns/	N-UNCOUNT Adolescence is the period of your life in which you develop from being a child into being an adult.	83
adolescent	/ˌædəˈlɛsənt/	N-COUNT Adolescent is used to describe young people who are no longer children but who have not yet become adults. It also refers to their behavior.	42, 83
algae	/ˈældʒi, ˈælgaɪ/	N-PLURAL Algae are plants with no stems or leaves that grow in water or on damp surfaces.	61
alleviate	/əˈliviˌeɪt/	N-UNCOUNT If you alleviate pain, suffering, or an unpleasant condition, you make it less intense or severe.	55, 98
animation	/ˌænɪˈmeɪʃən/	N-UNCOUNT Animation is the process of making films in which drawings or puppets appear to move.	58
anime	/ˈænɪmeɪ/	Japanese Style Animation	58
anorexia	/ˌænəˈrɛksiə/	N-UNCOUNT Anorexia or anorexia nervosa is an illness in which a person has an overwhelming fear of becoming fat, and so refuses to eat enough and becomes thinner and thinner.	45
ape	/eɪp/	N-COUNT Apes are chimpanzees, gorillas, and other animals in the same family. ...chimpanzees and other apes.	11
applaud	/əˈplɔd/	V-When a group of people applaud, they clap their hands in order to show approval, for example, when they have enjoyed a play or concert.	45
aquamarine	/ˌækwəməˈrin/	COLOR Aquamarine is used to describe things that are greenish-blue in color. ...warm aquamarine seas and white beaches.	53
aquatic	/əˈkwætɪk/	ADJ Aquatic means relating to water. An aquatic animal or plant lives or grows on or in water.	61
arctic	/ˈɑrktɪk/	N-PROPER The Arctic is the area of the world around the North Pole.	25
athlete	/ˈæθlit/	N-COUNT An athlete is a person who does any kind of physical sports, exercise, or games, especially in competitions.	9, 93 98
auburn	/ˈɔbərn/	COLOR Auburn hair is reddish brown.	53
authentic	/ɔˈθɛntɪk/	ADJ An authentic person, object, or emotion is genuine.	86
autobiography	/ˌɔtəbaɪˈɒgrəfi/	N-COUNT Your autobiography is an account of your life, which you write yourself.	14
avid	/ˈævɪd/	ADV You use avid to describe someone who is very enthusiastic about something that they do.	42
bamboo	/bæmˈbu/	N-VAR Bamboo is a tall tropical plant with hard, hollow stems. The young shoots of the plant can be eaten and the stems are used to make furniture.	114
beige	/beɪʒ/	COLOR Something that is beige is pale brown in color.	53
billboard	/ˈbɪlbɔrd/	N-COUNT A billboard is a very large board on which advertising is displayed.	45
billionaire	/ˌbɪliəˈnɛər/	N-COUNT A billionaire is an extremely rich person who has money or property worth at least a thousand million dollars.	39
bio-	/ˈbaɪoʊ-, baɪɒ-/	PREFIX Bio- is used at the beginning of nouns and adjectives that refer to life or to the study of living things. Therefore, biofuel is a substance produced from living things that can be burned to provide heat or power and biodiesel is a substance produced from living things that can replace the heavy fuel used in a diesel engine.	61, 98
biographer	/baɪˈɒgrəfər/	N-COUNT Someone's biographer is a person who writes an account of their life.	73

bloodstream	/blʌdstrim/	N-COUNT Your bloodstream is the blood that flows around your body.	117
blushing	/blʌʃɪŋ/	N-COUNT When you blush, your face becomes redder than usual because you are ashamed or embarrassed.	22
bracelet	/breɪslɪt/	N-COUNT A bracelet is a chain or band, usually made of metal, that you wear around your wrist as jewelry.	55
brunette	/brʌnɛt/	N-COUNT A brunette is a person, usually a woman or girl, with dark brown hair.	53
bulletin board	/bʌlɪtɪnbɔrd/	N-COUNT A bulletin board is a board that is usually attached to a wall in order to display notices giving information about something.	89
caffeine	/kæfin/	N-U Caffeine is a chemical substance found in coffee, tea, and cocoa, which affects your brain and body and makes you more active.	22
calorie	/kæləri/	N-COUNT Calories are units used to measure the energy value of food. People who are on diets try to eat food that does not contain many calories.	95
cherish	/tʃɛrɪʃ/	ADJ If you cherish something such as a pleasant memory, you keep it in your mind for a long period of time.	19
chimpanzee	/tʃɪmpænzi/	N-COUNT A chimpanzee (or chimp) is a kind of small African ape.	11
cinematography	/sɪnɪmətɒgrəfi/	N-UNCOUNT Cinematography is the technique of making movies.	17
cite	/saɪt/	V-T If you cite something, you quote it or mention it, especially as an example or proof of what you are saying.	58, 98, 114
classmate	/klæsmeɪt/	N-COUNT Your classmates are students who are in the same class as you at school or college.	14, 81
collateral	/kəlætərəl/	N-UNCOUNT Collateral is money or property which is used as a guarantee that someone will repay a loan.	114
coma	/koʊmə/	N-COUNT Someone who is in a coma is in a state of deep unconsciousness.	117
combustion	/kəmbʌstʃən/	N-UNCOUNT Combustion is the act of burning something or the process of burning.	61
complexion	/kəmplɛkʃən/	N-COUNT When you refer to someone's complexion, you are referring to the natural color or condition of the skin on their face.	53
compulsive	/kəmpʌlsɪv/	ADJ You use compulsive to describe people or their behavior when they cannot stop doing something wrong, harmful, or unnecessary.	93
conversely	/kɒnvɛrsli/	ADV You say conversely to indicate that the situation you are about to describe is the opposite or reverse of the one you have just described.	50
counteract	/kaʊntərækt/	V-T To counteract something means to reduce its effect by doing something that produces an opposite effect.	81
counterproductive	/kaʊntərprədʌctɪv/	ADJ Something that is counterproductive achieves the opposite result from the one that you want to achieve.	81
cubicle	/kyubɪkəl/	N-COUNT A cubicle is an area in an office that is separated from the rest of the room by thin walls.	95
cue	/kyu/	N-COUNT If you say that something that happens is a cue for an action, you mean that people start doing that action when it happens.	95
Cyber bullying	/saɪbəbʊliɪŋ/	N-UNCOUNT Cyber bullying involves using the Internet to threaten, hurt, or frighten another person, especially by sending threatening or insulting messages.	89
daydream	/deɪdrim/	V-I If you daydream, you think about pleasant things for a period of time, usually about things that you would like to happen.	37
decor	/deɪkɔr/	N-UNCOUNT The decor of a house or room is its style of furnishing and decoration.	55
default	/dɪfɔlt/	N-UNCOUNT If a person, company, or country defaults on something that they have legally agreed to do, such as paying some money or doing a piece of work, they fail to do it.	114
deforestation	/difɔrɪsteɪʃən/	N-UNCOUNT If an area is deforested, all the trees there are cut down or destroyed. One percent of Brazil's total forest cover is being lost every year to deforestation.	61
dependence	/dɪpɛndəns/	N-UNCOUNT Your dependence on something or someone is your need for them in order to succeed or be able to survive.	61

depict	/dɪpɪkt/	V-T To depict someone or something means to show or represent them in a work of art such as a drawing or painting.	50
detergent	/dɪtɛrdʒənt/	N-MASS Detergent is a chemical substance, usually in the form of a powder or liquid used for washing things such as clothes or dishes.	50
diligent	/dɪlɪdʒənt/	ADV Someone who is diligent works hard in a careful and thorough way.	83
dissection	/dɪsɛktʃn/	N-VAR If someone dissects the body of a dead person or animal, they carefully cut it up in order to examine it scientifically.	86
download	/daʊnloʊd/	V-T To download data means to transfer it to or from a computer along a line such as a telephone line, a radio link, or a computer network.	86
elusive	/ɪlusɪv/	ADJ Something or someone that is elusive is difficult to find, describe, remember, or achieve.	33
embody	/ɪmbʊdi/	V-T To embody an idea or quality means to be a symbol or expression of that idea or quality.	58
emission	/ɪmɪʃən/	N-VAR An emission of something such as gas or radiation is the release of it into the atmosphere.	61
ethical	/ɛθɪkəl/	ADV Ethical means relating to beliefs about right and wrong. If you describe something as ethical, you mean that it is morally right or morally acceptable.	30, 70, 89, 103
etiquette	/ɛtɪkɪt, –kɛt/	N-UNCOUNT Etiquette is a set of customs and rules for polite behavior, especially among a particular class of people or in a particular profession.	67
exhilarating	/ɪgzɪləreɪtɪŋ/	ADJ If you describe an experience or feeling as exhilarating, you mean that it makes you feel very happy and excited.	22
exile	/ɛksaɪl/	N-UNCOUNT If someone is living in exile, they are living in a foreign country because they cannot live in their own country, usually for political reasons. V-T If someone is exiled, they are living in a foreign country because they cannot live in their own country, usually for political reasons. N-COUNT An exile is someone who has been exiled.	17, 19
faculty	/fækəlti/	N-VAR A faculty is all the teaching staff of a university or college, or of one department.	86
famine	/fæmɪn/	N-VAR Famine is a situation in which large numbers of people have little or no food, and many of them die.	114
fatigue	/fətig/	N-UNCOUNT Fatigue is a feeling of extreme physical or mental tiredness.	117
fearsome	/fɪərsɒm/	ADJ Fearsome is used to describe things that are frightening, for example, because of their large size or extreme nature.	25
feat	/fɪt/	N-COUNT If you refer to an action, or the result of an action, as a feat, you admire it because it is an impressive and difficult achievement.	33
figurine	/fɪgyərɪn/	N-COUNT A figurine is a small, decorative model of a person.	58
first hand	/fɛrst hænd/	ADV First hand information or experience is gained or learned directly, rather than from other people or from books.	114
foresight	/fɔresaɪt/	N-UNCOUNT Someone's foresight is their ability to see what is likely to happen in the future and to take appropriate action.	39
fossil-fuel	/fɒsəl fyuel/	N-MASS Fossil fuel is fuel such as coal or oil that is formed from the decayed remains of plants or animals.	61
fraudulent	/frɔdʒələnt/	ADV A fraudulent activity is deliberately deceitful, dishonest, or untrue.	42
freckle	/frɛkəl/	N-COUNT Freckles are small light brown spots on someone's skin, especially on their face.	53
frugal	/frugəl/	N-UNCOUNT People who are frugal or who live frugal lives do not spend much money on themselves.	39
geeky	/giki/	ADJ If you describe someone as geeky, you think they look or behave like a geek, someone who is skilled with computers, and who seems more interested in them than in people, or someone, usually a man or boy, awkward, or weak.	86

genetic	/dʒɪnɛtɪk/	ADV You use genetic to describe something that is concerned with genetics or with genes.	22, 33
gluttony	/glʌtəni/	N-UNCOUNT Gluttony is the act or habit of eating too much or being greedy.	93
goodwill ambassador	/gʊdwɪl æmbæsədər/	N-COUNT A goodwill ambassador represents and promotes friendly or helpful attitudes and ideas toward other people, countries, or organizations.	103
greenhouse gasses	/grinhaʊs gæsɪs/	N-VAR the gases responsible for causing the greenhouse effect. The main greenhouse gas is carbon dioxide.	61
hardwired	/hɑrdwaɪərd/	ADJ If an ability, approach, or type of activity is hardwired into the brain, it is a basic one and cannot be changed.	22
heartbeat	/hɑrtbit/	N-SING Your heartbeat is the regular movement of your heart as it pumps blood around your body.	55
heartbreaking	/hɑrtbreɪkɪŋ/	ADJ Something that is heartbreaking makes you feel extremely sad and upset.	17, 30
heartwarming	/hɑrtwɔrmɪŋ/	ADJ Something that is heartwarming causes you to feel happy, usually because something nice has happened to people.	30
hesitant	/hɛzɪtənt/	ADV If you are hesitant about doing something, you do not do it quickly or immediately, usually because you are uncertain, embarrassed, or worried.	19
Hindu	/hɪndu/	N-COUNT A Hindu is a person who believes in Hinduism and follows its teachings. ADJ Hindu is used to describe things that belong or relate to Hinduism.	55, 67
Hinduism	/hɪnduɪzəm/	N-UNCOUNT Hinduism is an Indian religion. It has many gods and teaches that people have another life on earth after they die.	67
Hispanic	/hɪspænɪk/	N-COUNT A Hispanic person is a citizen of the United States of America who originally came from Latin America, or whose family originally came from Latin America.	67
HIV	/eɪtʃ aɪ vi/	N-UNCOUNT HIV is a virus which reduces people's resistance to illness and can cause AIDS. HIV is an abbreviation for `human immunodeficiency virus.'	27, 106
humanitarian	/hjumænɪtɛəriən/	ADJ If a person or society has humanitarian ideas or behavior, they try to avoid making people suffer or they help people who are suffering.	98, 106
immune system	/ɪmyun sɪstəm/	N-COUNT Your immune system consists of all the organs and processes in your body that protect you from illness and infection.	33
incubation	/ɪnkyəbeɪʃən/	N-UNCOUNT When birds incubate their eggs, or when they incubate, they keep the eggs warm until the baby birds come out.	117
infusion	/ɪnfyuʒən/	N-VAR If there is an infusion of one thing into another, the first thing is added to the other thing and makes it stronger or better.	58
innovative	/ɪnəveɪtɪv/	V-I To innovate means to introduce changes and new ideas in the way something is done or made.	86, 111
insecticide	/ɪnsɛktɪsaɪd/	N-MASS Insecticide is a chemical substance that is used to kill insects.	117
insomnia	/ɪnsɒmniə/	N-U Someone who suffers from insomnia finds it difficult to sleep.	81
intercontinental	/ɪntərkɒntɪnɛntəl/	ADJ Intercontinental is used to describe something that exists or happens between continents.	65
interpersonal	/ɪntərpɜrsənəl/	ADJ Interpersonal means relating to relationships between people.	9, 14
intrapersonal	/ɪntrəpɜrsənəl/	ADJ Intrapersonal means relating to the internal aspects of a person, their mind or self, having an understanding of yourself.	9, 14
IQ	/aɪ kyu/	N-VAR Your IQ is your level of intelligence, as indicated by a special test that you do. IQ is an abbreviation for `intelligence quotient'.	14
Islamic	/ɪslæmɪk/	ADJ Islamic means belonging or relating to Islam, the religion of the Muslims, which was started by Mohammed.	55
ivory color	/aɪvəri cʌlər/	COLOR Ivory is a creamy-white color.	53
kerosene	/kɛrəsin/	N-UNCOUNT Kerosene is a clear, strong-smelling liquid which is used as a fuel, for example in heaters and lamps.	61

kindhearted	/kaɪndhɑrtɪd/	ADJ If you describe someone as kind-hearted, you mean that they are kind, caring, and generous.	27
kinesthetic	/kinɛsθɛtɪk/	ADJ Relating to movement.	9
lavender	/lævɪndər/	ADJ Lavender is a bluish-purple color.	53
legend	/lɛdʒənd/	N-COUNT If you refer to someone as a legend, you mean that they are very famous and admired by a lot of people.	106
linguistic	/lɪŋgwɪstɪk/	ADJ Linguistic abilities or ideas relate to language or linguistics.	9, 14
lotion	/ləʊʃən/	N-MASS A lotion is a liquid that you use to clean, improve, or protect your skin or hair. E.g. suntan lotion.	70
lucrative	/lukrətɪv/	ADJ A lucrative activity, job, or business deal is very profitable.	30
lunar	/lunər /	ADJ Lunar means relating to the moon.	55
malarial	/məlɛəriəl/	N-UNCOUNT Malaria is a serious disease carried by mosquitoes which causes periods of fever. ADJ You can use malarial to refer to things connected with malaria or areas which are affected by malaria.	27, 117
malnutrition	/mælnutrɪʃən/	N-U If someone is suffering from malnutrition, they are physically weak and extremely thin because they have not eaten enough food.	98
Manga	/mæŋgə/	N-UNCOUNT Manga is a style of drawing, originally from Japan, that is used in comic books.	58
meager	/migər/	ADJ If you describe an amount or quantity of something as meager, you are critical of it because it is very small or not enough.	98
meditating	/mɛdɪteɪʃən/	V-I If you meditate you remain in a silent and calm state for a period of time, as part of a religious training or so that you are more able to deal with the problems and difficulties of everyday life.	33
metabolism	/mɪtæbəlizəm/	N-VAR Your metabolism is the way that chemical processes in your body cause food to be used in an efficient way, for example to make new cells and to give you energy.	55
monologue	/mɒnəlɔg/	N-VAR A monologue is a long speech which is spoken by one person as an entertainment, or as part of an entertainment such as a play.	17
mosaic	/moʊzeɪɪk/	N-VAR A mosaic is a design which consists of small pieces of colored glass, pottery, or stone set in concrete or plaster.	55
mosque	/mɒsk/	N-COUNT A mosque is a building where Muslims go to worship.	55
mosquito	/mɒskitəʊ/	N-COUNT Mosquitoes are small flying insects which bite people and animals in order to suck their blood.	117
multimedia	/mʌltimidiə/	N-UNCOUNT You use multimedia to refer to computer programs and products which involve sound, pictures, and film, as well as text. In education, multimedia is the use of television and other different media in a lesson, as well as books.	9
Muslim	/mʌslɪm/	N-COUNT A Muslim is someone who believes in Islam and lives according to its rules. ADJ Muslim means relating to Islam or Muslims.	55, 67
mute	/myut/	ADV Someone who is mute is silent for a particular reason and does not speak. He was mute, distant, and indifferent.	14
muted color	/ myutɪd cʌlər/	ADJ Muted colors are soft and gentle, not bright and strong.	53, 67
narration	/næreɪʃən/	N-COUNT If you narrate a story, you tell it from your own point of view. Its story-within-a-story method of narration is confusing.	50
necklace	/nɛklɪs/	N-COUNT A necklace is a piece of jewelry such as a chain or a string of beads which someone, usually a woman, wears around their neck.	55
neckline	/nɛklaɪn/	N-COUNT The neckline of a dress, blouse, or other piece of clothing is the edge that goes around your neck, especially the front part of it.	67
needy	/nidi/	N-PLURAL Needy people do not have enough food, medicine, or clothing, or adequate houses.	106
nude	/nud/	PHRASE A nude person is not wearing any clothes.	45
nurturing	/nɜrtʃərɪŋ/	V-T If you nurture something such as a young child or a young plant, you care for it while it is growing and developing. N-UNCOUNT Nurture is care and encouragement that is given to someone while they are growing and developing.	27

nutrition	/nutrɪʃən/	N-UNCOUNT Nutrition is the process of taking food into the body and absorbing the nutrients in those foods.	50, 106, 114
nutritious	/nutrɪʃəs/	ADJ Nutritious food contains substances which help your body to be healthy.	98
obesity	/əʊbisɪti/	N-UNCOUNT If someone is obese, they are extremely fat.	93
odorless	/əʊdərlɪs/	ADJ An odorless substance has no smell.	22
offspring	/ɔfsprɪŋ/	N-COUNT You can refer to a person's children or to an animal's young as their offspring. Offspring is both the singular and the plural form.	11, 22
olive (color)	/ɒlɪv/	ADJ If someone has olive skin, the color of their skin is yellowish brown.	53
ominously	/ɒmɪnəsli/	ADV If you describe something as ominous, you mean that it worries you because it makes you think that something bad is going to happen. Ominously. The room seemed ominously quiet.	30
optimism	/ɒptɪmɪzəm/	N-UNCOUNT Optimism is the feeling of being hopeful about the future or about the success of something in particular.	39
orphanage	/ɔrfənɪdʒ/	N-C An orphanage is a place where orphans live and are cared for.	27, 30
outspoken	/aʊtspoʊkən/	N-UNCOUNT Someone who is outspoken gives their opinions about things openly and honestly, even if they are likely to shock or offend people.	19
outweigh	/aʊtweɪ/	V-T If one thing outweighs another, the first thing is of greater importance, benefit, or significance than the second thing.	81
overburdened	/əʊvərbɜrdənd/	ADJ If a system or organization is overburdened, it has too many people or things to deal with and so does not function properly.	81
parasite	/pærəsaɪt/	N-COUNT A parasite is a small animal or plant that lives on or inside a larger animal or plant, and gets its food from it.	117
password	/pæswɜrd/	N-COUNT A password is a secret word or phrase that you must know in order to be allowed to enter a place such as a military base, or to be allowed to use a computer system.	89
pastel	/pæstɛl/	N-COUNT Pastel colors are pale rather than dark or bright.	53
peach (color)	/pitʃ/	ADJ Something that is peach is pale pinky-orange in color.	53
per capita	/pər kæpɪtə/	ADV The per capita amount of something is the total amount of it in a country or area divided by the number of people in that country or area.	14, 109
peripheral	/pərɪfərəl/	ADJ A peripheral activity or issue is one that is not very important compared with other activities or issues.	47
perpetrator	/pɜrpɪtreɪtə/	N-COUNT If someone perpetrates a crime or any other immoral or harmful act, they do it.	89
petroleum	/pətrəʊliəm/	N-UNCOUNT Petroleum is oil that is found under the surface of the earth or under the sea bed. Gasoline and kerosene are obtained from petroleum.	61
photosynthesis	/fəʊtəʊsɪnθəsɪs/	N-UNCOUNT Photosynthesis is the way that green plants make their food using sunlight.	61
physiological	/fɪzɪɒlɒdʒɪkəl/	ADJ The physiology of a human or animal's body or of a plant is the way that it functions.	95
popcorn	/pɒpkɔrn/	N-UNCOUNT Popcorn is a snack that consists of grains of corn that have been heated until they have burst and become large and light.	95
prepaid	/pripeɪd/	ADJ Prepaid items are paid for in advance, before the time when you would normally pay for them.	39, 111
primate	/praɪmeɪt/	N-COUNT A primate is a member of the group of mammals that includes humans, monkeys, and apes.	11
proactive	/prəʊæktɪv/	ADJ Proactive actions are intended to cause changes, rather than just reacting to change.	89, 117
proclaim	/prəʊkleɪm/	V-T If you proclaim something, you state it in a forceful way.	37
psychedelic	/saɪkədɛlɪk/	ADJ Psychedelic art has bright colors and strange patterns.	58

psychotherapist	/saɪkəʊθɛrəpɪst/	N-COUNT A psychotherapist is a person who treats people who are mentally ill using psychotherapy, the use of psychological methods in treating people who are mentally ill, rather than using physical methods such as drugs or surgery.	89
publicist	/pʌblɪsɪst/	N-COUNT A publicist is a person whose job involves getting publicity for people, events, or things such as movies or books.	58
punctual	/pʌŋktʃʊəl/	ADV If you are punctual, you do something or arrive somewhere at the right time and are not late.	67
radiant	/reɪdiənt/	ADJ Someone who is radiant is so happy that their happiness shows in their face.	53
recipient	/rɪsɪpiənt/	N-COUNT The recipient of something is the person who receives it.	111
reckless	/rɛklɪs/	N-UNCOUNT If you say that someone is reckless, you mean that they act in a way which shows that they do not care about danger or the effect their behavior will have.	103
reinforce	/riɪnfɔrs/	V-T If something reinforces an idea or point of view, it provides more evidence or support for it.	81, 83
repetitive	/rɪpɛtɪtɪv/	ADJ Something that is repetitive involves actions or elements that are repeated many times and is therefore boring.	83
replicate	/rɛplɪkeɪt/	V-T If you replicate someone's experiment, work, or research, you do it yourself in exactly the same way.	30, 86
repository	/rɪpɒzɪtɔri/	N-COUNT A repository is a place where something is kept safely.	22
revere	/rɪvɪər/	ADJ If you revere someone or something, you respect and admire them greatly.	67
rickshaw	/rɪkʃɔ/	N-COUNT A rickshaw is a simple vehicle that is used in Asia for carrying passengers. Some rickshaws are pulled by a man who walks or runs in front.	106
rigors	/rɪgərz/	N-PLURAL The rigors of an activity or job are the difficult, demanding, or unpleasant things that are associated with it.	83
run-down	/rʌn daʊn/	ADJ A run-down building or area is in very poor condition.	101
saliva	/səlaɪvə/	N-UNCOUNT Saliva is the watery liquid that forms in your mouth and helps you to chew and digest food.	22
salivary gland	/sælɪvɛri glænd/	N-COUNT Your salivary glands are the glands that produce saliva in your mouth.	117
sanitation	/sænɪteɪʃən/	N-UNCOUNT Sanitation is the process of keeping places clean and healthy, especially by providing a sewage system and a clean water supply.	106
scent	/sɛnt/	N-COUNT The scent of something is the smell that it has, usually pleasant.	22
seizure	/siʒər/	N-COUNT If someone has a seizure, they have a sudden violent attack of an illness, especially one that affects their heart or brain.	117
setback	/sɛtbæk/	N-COUNT A setback is an event that delays your progress or reverses some of the progress that you have made.	39
shrimp	/ʃrɪmp/	N-COUNT Shrimps are small shellfish with long tails and many legs.	65
sibling	/sɪblɪŋ/	N-COUNT Your siblings are your brothers and sisters.	27
skeptical	/skɛptɪkəl/	ADJ If you are skeptical about something, you have doubts about it.	61
smuggle	/smʌgəl/	N-UNCOUNT If someone smuggles things or people into a place or out of it, they take them there illegally or secretly. My message is "If you try to smuggle drugs you are stupid."	103
soothe	/suð/	ADJ Something that soothes a part of your body where there is pain or discomfort makes the pain or discomfort less severe.	55
spatial	/speɪʃəl/	ADJ Spatial is used to describe things relating to areas. ADJ Your spatial ability is your ability to see and understand the relationships between shapes, spaces, and areas.	9, 14
spectator	/spɛkteɪtər/	N-COUNT A spectator is someone who watches something, especially a sports event.	93, 106
spendthrift	/spɛndθrɪft/	ADJ If you call someone a spendthrift, you mean that they spend too much money.	39

spokesperson	/spoʊkspɜrsən/	N-COUNT A spokesperson is a person who speaks as the representative of a group or organization.	27
stale	/steɪl/	ADJ Stale food is no longer fresh or good to eat.	95
subdued	/səbdud/	ADJ Subdued lights or colors are not very bright. The lighting was subdued.	53
suburb	/sʌbɜrb/	N-COUNT A suburb of a city or large town is a smaller area which is part of the city or large town but is outside its center.	101
suppress	/səprɛs/	N-UNCOUNT If a natural function or reaction of your body is suppressed, it is stopped, for example by drugs or illness.	55
sway	/sweɪ/	V-I When people or things sway, they lean or swing slowly from one side to the other.	37
sweater	/swɛtər/	N-COUNT A sweater is a warm knitted piece of clothing which covers the upper part of your body and your arms.	111
symmetrical	/sɪmɛtrɪkəl/	ADV If something is symmetrical, it has two halves which are exactly the same, except that one half is the mirror image of the other.	22
testosterone	/tɛstɒstəroʊn/	N-UNCOUNT Testosterone is a hormone found in men and male animals, which can also be produced artificially.	22
text messaging	/tɛkst mɛsɪdʒ/	N-UNCOUNT Text messaging is the sending of written messages using a cell phone.	111
textbook	/tɛkstbʊk/	N-COUNT A textbook is a book containing facts about a particular subject that is used by people studying that subject.	86
thatched	/θætʃt/	ADJ A thatched house or a house with a thatched roof has a roof made of straw or reeds.	27
thereby	/ðɛərbaɪ/	ADV You use thereby to introduce an important result or consequence of the event or action you have just mentioned.	75
thrive	/θraɪv/	V-I If someone or something thrives, they do well and are successful, healthy, or strong.	70
toothpaste	/tʊθpaɪst/	N-MASS Toothpaste is a thick substance which you put on your toothbrush and use to clean your teeth.	61
trafficking	/træfɪkɪŋ/	N-UNCOUNT Someone who traffics in something such as drugs or stolen goods buys and sells them even though it is illegal to do so.	27, 70, 103
trait	/treɪt/	N-COUNT A trait is a particular characteristic, quality, or tendency that someone or something has.	22, 39
transform	/trænsfɔrm/	N-VAR To transform something into something else means to change or convert it into that thing.	111
tribe	/traɪb/	N-COUNT-COLL Tribe is sometimes used to refer to a group of people of the same race, language, and customs, especially in a developing country. Some people disapprove of this use.	22
triumphant	/traɪʌmfənt/	ADV Someone who is triumphant has gained a victory or succeeded in something and feels very happy about it.	93
underachiever	/ʌndərətʃivər/	N-COUNT If someone underachieves in something such as schoolwork or a job, they do not perform as well as they could.	9
utensil	/yutɛnsəl/	N-COUNT Utensils are tools or objects that you use in order to help you to cook, serve food, or eat.	95
vendor	/vɛndər/	N-COUNT A vendor is someone who sells things such as newspapers or food from a small stall or cart.	114
veteran	/vɛtərən/	N-COUNT You use veteran to refer to someone who has been involved in a particular activity for a long time.	83
voice-over	/vɔɪsoʊvər/	N-COUNT The voice-over of a film, television program, or advertisement consists of words spoken by someone who is not seen.	50
weatherproof	/wɛðərpruf/	ADJ Something that is weatherproof is made of material that protects it from the weather or keeps out wind and rain.	111
worksheet	/wɜrkʃit/	N-COUNT A specially prepared page of exercises designed to improve your knowledge or understanding of a particular subject.	83
yarn	/yɑrn/	N-MASS Yarn is thread used for knitting or making cloth.	111

Reading Strategies Index

Unit 1
Reading 1: Skimming (2), Highlighting/Recognizing main ideas (4), Annotating (5)
Reading 2: Skimming (1), Scanning (2), Annotating (3), Highlighting (5), Making inferences (6)

Unit 2
Reading 1: Skimming/Recognizing tone (1), Understanding purpose (2) Making associations (4) Separating fact from opinion (6)
Reading 2: Skimming/Understanding purpose (1), Annotating (2) Summarizing/Separating fact from opinion (5), Making interpretations (6)

Unit 3
Reading 1: Making associations (1), Skimming/Recognizing purpose (2), Recognizing bias (3, 4), Understanding references (5)
Reading 2: Skimming/Highlighting/Recognizing main ideas (1), Scanning (2) Recognizing bias/Annotating (4), Recognizing tone (5), Identifying bias (6) Separating fact from opinion (8)

Review 1
Reading Strategies: Understanding purpose (2), Recognizing tone (3), Annotating (4)
Comprehension Check: Making inferences (5)
More Word Chunks: Associating (2)

Unit 4
Reading 1: Associating (1), Skimming/Recognizing main ideas (2), Improving Fluency (3, 5, 8), Highlighting (6), Making inferences (7)
Reading 2: Associating (1), Scanning/Highlighting (2), Improving Fluency (3, 5), Associating (4) Associating (6) Recognizing bias (8)

Unit 5
Reading 1: Skimming/Recognizing main idea (1), Improving fluency (2, 4) Synthesizing information (6)
Reading 2: Skimming/Recognizing main ideas (2), Visualizing (3, 4), Recognizing main ideas (5), Making judgments (6)

Unit 6
Reading 1: Associating (1), Improving fluency (2, 4), Highlighting (3) Associating (5) Summarizing (7)
Reading 2: Skimming/Recognizing main ideas (1), Making judgments (3), Separating fact from opinion (4), Making inferences (5), Summarizing (6)

Review 2
Reading Strategies: Skimming, Recognizing main ideas (2), Improving fluency (3), Summarizing (4), Making judgments (5)
Comprehension Check: Making inferences (6)
More Word Chunks: Improving fluency (1-3)

Unit 7
Reading 1: Making Associations (1), Skimming/Recognizing purpose (2), Identifying text organization (3), Associating (4), Synthesizing information (5), Highlighting (6), Summarizing (7)
Reading 2: Scanning (1), Skimming/Recognizing main ideas (2), Identifying text organization/Highlighting (3), Summarizing (5), Scanning/Deducing meaning (6)

Unit 8
Reading 1: Associating (1), Skimming, Recognizing main ideas (2), Making interpretations (3), Identifying text organizations (4), Associating (5)
Reading 2: Associating (1), Skimming/Recognizing main ideas (2), Highlighting (3), Recognizing text organization (4), Synthesizing information (5), Making judgments (6)

Unit 9
Reading 1: Associating (1), Skimming/Recognizing main ideas (2), Highlighting (3) Synthesizing information (5)
Reading 2: Associating (1), Improving fluency (2, 3, 4), Summarizing (5), Recognizing bias (6), Separating fact from opinion (7), Making inferences (8)

Review 3
Reading Strategies: Recognizing text organization (1), Skimming/Recognizing main ideas (2), Recognizing text organization (3), Separating fact from opinion (4), Summarizing (5)
Comprehension Check: Improving fluency (1-5)
More Word Chunks: Improving fluency (1-3)

Unit 10
Reading 1: Associating (1), Visualizing (2) Summarizing (4), Synthesizing information (5), Improving fluency (6)
Reading 2: Skimming/Recognizing main ideas (1), Improving fluency (2, 3, 4), Recognizing purpose (6)

Unit 11
Reading 1: Skimming/Recognizing main ideas (1), Highlighting (2), Making judgments (3), Understanding references (4), Improving fluency (5), Skimming (6)
Reading 2: Associating (1), Skimming/Recognizing main ideas (2), Improving fluency (3), Highlighting (4), Understanding references (5)

Unit 12
Reading 1: Visualizing (2), Associating (3), Synthesizing information (4), Summarizing (5)
Reading 2: Skimming (2); Cause and effect (2); Annotating (3); Making assoSkimming/Recognizing main ideas (1), Improving fluency (2), Separating fact from opinion (3), Synthesizing information (5)

Review 4
Reading Strategies Review: Scanning (2), Deducing meaning (3), Understanding references (4), Synthesizing information (5)
Comprehension Check: Making inferences (5)
More Word Chunks: Improving fluency (1-3)